Beware the Stranger

Chiasma 13

General Editor

Michael Bishop

Editorial Committee

Adelaide Russo, Michael Sheringham
Steven Winspur, Sonya Stephens
Michael Brophy, Anja Pearre

Amsterdam - New York, NY 2002

Beware the Stranger

The Survenant *in the Quebec Novel*

Peter Noble

Le papier sur lequel le présent ouvrage est imprimé remplit les prescriptions de "ISO 9706:1994, Information et documentation - Papier pour documents - Prescriptions pour la permanence".

The paper on which this book is printed meets the requirements of "ISO 9706:1994, Information and documentation - Paper for documents - Requirements for permanence".

ISBN: 90-420-0913-6
©Editions Rodopi B.V., Amsterdam - New York, NY 2002
Printed in The Netherlands

CHIASMA

Chiasma seeks to foster urgent critical assessments focussing upon joinings and crisscrossings, single, triangular, multiple, in the realm of modern French literature. Studies may be of an interdisciplinary nature, developing connections with art, philosophy, linguistics and beyond, or display intertextual or other plurivocal concerns of varying order.

Michael Bishop
Halifax, 2002

*

In this book, Peter Noble pursues a common thread running through five prominent novels published in Quebec in the last half century: the theme of a disruptive newcomer in a community. Peculiarly suited to Quebec tradition, the modern *survenant* or *survenante* has partly assumed the role of the historic *coureur de bois* whose unfettered energy not only relieved the boredom but frequently threatened the delicate social balance of any settlement he was passing through. Whether wreaking havoc or bringing a breath of fresh air, the *survenant* can be a catalyst for startling revelations and irrevocable change. As Noble shows with admirable detail, Guèvremont, Langevin, Bessette, Hébert and Hamelin offer widely differing views of the clash between the predictable world of the sedentary and the chaotic one of the uprooted.

Anja Pearre
Halifax, 2002

Table of Contents

Preface	9
From *coureur de bois* to *survenant*	10
The Idea of the survenant	17
Le Survenant; Germaine Guèvremont	21
Poussière sur la ville; André Langevin	40
Le Libraire; Gérard Bessette	62
Les Fous de Bassan; Anne Hébert	73
Cowboy; Louis Hamelin	93
Conclusion	110
Select Bibliography	113

Preface

This book is the product of reading and teaching Quebec literature over many years at the University of Reading during which time I have enjoyed the work of many Quebec writers in addition to those who are mentioned in this book. I hope that I will make one of the most vibrant and exciting of contemporary literatures a little better known to a public which, in the main, is completely unaware of the extent and the richness of twentieth century Quebec writing. Many people have helped me in the course of my work, and I am grateful to the University of Reading and the British Academy whose grants enabled me to travel to Montreal to carry out research on the spot. I am particularly grateful to Guy Laflèche of the Université de Montréal for years of encouragement and support, to Micheline Cambron and her staff at the Centre d'Études Québécoises at the same university for their helpfulness and courtesy, to the staff of the Union des écrivains québécois who were extremely kind to me, to Jacques Allard for his helpful advice and to Gwen Newsham for her hospitality and support. I am grateful to Michael Bishop for accepting the book and for all his encouragement. I would also like to thank my colleagues at the University of Reading for their support and their comments on various drafts of the chapters which were given as research papers to the Departmental Research Group. I could not have completed the formatting of the book without the help of Tony Simons and Judi Upton-Ward Above all I would like to thank my wife for patiently reading and correcting the draft typescript and, in particular, Professor Walter Redfern who read and commented on the whole book. Anja Pearre has been a most sympathetic and helpful editor, and I am extremely grateful to her for her patient support. Their help has made it a much better book, but they are in no way responsible for any defects that remain.

From *coureur de bois* to *survenant*

The history of the settlement of Canada by the French and the social structures which emerged during the period of French dominance favoured the concept of the nomadic adventurer who paused briefly in a settlement before moving on to the next challenge, as Fernand Dumont explains (65).

> Dès les débuts de la Nouvelle-France, le *coureur des bois* est un personnage à part. N'éprouvant pas d'intérêt pour les travaux agricoles, peu préoccupé des autorités qui règnent dans les villes, il s'enfonce dans la forêt en quête d'un commerce qu'il mène à sa guise; il y adopte plus ou moins les mœurs des Indiens, apprend les langues indigènes, obéit à ses propres normes. Souvent contrebandier mal vu par les administrateurs et les prêtres, il abandonne sa marchandise et ses services au plus offrant, fût-il de New York plutôt que de Montréal ou Québec.

The early history of Canada is filled with famous names, such as La Salle, Radisson and La Vérendrye, who carried the French flag south, north and west from its base in the Saint Lawrence valley. The importance of La Vérendrye, in particular in the push westwards, is emphasised by Yves Frenette (19).

> Ainsi, entre 1728 et 1743, La Vérendrye et ses compagnons établissent un réseau de postes dans l'Ouest canadien et américain, tel le Grand Portage dans l'actuel Minnesota, rendez-vous de traite des voyageurs et des Amérindiens.

These men frequently worked closely with the local authorities despite the disapproval of the distant royal government which short-sightedly demanded a greater concentration on the profitable fur trade rather than on expensive and pointless journeys into the unmapped regions of remote Indian tribes, as is shown by Michelle Lavoie in her important article on the *coureur de bois* (16). She also points out that such men had a recognised place in their society which was the starting and finishing point for their explorations (17-19). They returned to their community after each expedition to report back, to rest and to re-equip before starting the next adventure. The government in Paris might disapprove of these independent-minded, restless adventurers, but the local governor knew their worth as spies, informants and negotiators with the Indian tribes. Their heyday was the eighteenth century when the French still ruled in what is now Canada, when settlement was very much concentrated along the valley of the Saint Lawrence and the French adventurers could plunge into the excitement of life with the Indians away from European civilisation and the control of the church and royal power. Although many such men 'went Indian', marrying Indian women and settling amongst them, many did not and regularly returned to their base, where they were a recognised part of the social structure. Dumont has shown that towards the end of the seventeenth century the *coureurs de bois* were replaced under the pressure of events by men whose specialised function in their society was recognised and who were given the official status of *voyageurs* (65-66).

> Son [le *coureur de bois*] statut se modifie avec l'intensification du trafic et les nécessités de l'organisation. En 1681, on accorde officiellement une amnistie aux coureurs des bois; on institue des permis de traite, des «congés». Ceux-ci sont attribués à un chef d'expédition ou à un marchand qui organise et finance les entreprises. Alors apparaît le «voyageur», un spécialiste promis à une carrière de longue durée.

In the time of the *coureurs de bois* the settlers had vast areas of the continent to explore and claim for La Nouvelle-France. By the late seventeenth and early eighteenth centuries France had claimed and had colonised Acadie and the Saint Lawrence basin. In 1682 La Salle had reached the Caribbean, to the alarm of the Spaniards, and claimed the whole of the Mississippi drainage for France. The line of French forts stretched from Fort Frontenac on Lake Ontario out west to the Mississippi valley and then south to Fort Maurepas on the Caribbean, protecting the French settlers and explorers and hemming in the expansionist British and Spanish.[1] The importance of the fur trade in the early economy of Nouvelle-France had a decisive influence on the young colony. Politics and commerce combined to make control of the waterways essential, as Frenette points out (15).

> Le réseau hydrographique donnant seul accès aux réservoirs de fourrures, la France doit en assurer le contrôle. Les impératifs du commerce rejoignent ainsi les visées géostratégiques de la métropole. En effet, comme ses rivales sont aussi présentes dans le Nouveau Monde, la France doit y établir une territorialité et y faire valoir ses droits pour maintenir son prestige en Europe.

---

[1] *The Times Atlas of World History*, edited by Geoffrey Barraclough, London: Times Books, 1978, p.161

This riverine access to new territories was essential as ruthless overhunting killed off the fur-bearing animals in the more accessible lands which had been settled or explored in the early years of the colony. According to Frenette the wealth to be gained from the fur trade was almost the only aspect of Nouvelle-France that interested the royal government in Europe (14).

> La Nouvelle-France ne recelant ni or, ni argent ni denrée exotique, il n'y a guère que la fourrure qui intéresse le royaume de France, une exigence qui va peser lourd sur l'évolution de la colonie. Pendant trois quarts de siècle, le roi donne la Nouvelle-France en monopole à de grands personnages et à des compagnies de traite, dont Champlain est le premier gérant.

The riches to be gained in the fur trade meant that agriculture was slow to develop in the new colony and tended to remain at subsistence level. Exploration as far west as the Rockies was encouraged, so that the tradition was quickly established of the roaming adventurer as one of the main figures of the French community in the New World.

The defeat of Montcalm outside the walls of Quebec in 1759 was followed in 1763 by the Treaty of Paris which ended France's ambitions in North America. Quebec and all French possessions east of the Mississippi were surrendered to Britain, and Louisiana west of the Mississippi was surrendered to Spain. The French who stayed in North America were henceforth to be ruled by a foreign power, speaking a different language. Yves Frenette sums up the changes that this brought about (39).

> Dans le long terme: passage d'une économie fondée sur la traite à une économie agricole. Et dans un contexte de contact avec un Autre supérieur en nombre et en prestige: anglicisation; migrations liées à la socioéconomie continentale et régionale changeante, ainsi qu'à la mouvance des frontières politiques; transferts culturels et ethnogénèse.

For the most part the French-Canadians found themselves deprived of the status and independence that they had previously enjoyed. They had to work for wealthy anglophones, were controlled by anglophone courts and had lost most of their natural leaders of the seigniorial class, the majority of whose members had returned to France after the Conquest. The members of the class who remained in North America had to adapt to the new British rulers and had to compromise to ensure their survival. The difficulties of their position are summarised by Dumont (112).

> La noblesse qui demeure au pays aux lendemains de la conquête se réduit à un groupe de seigneurs et coseigneurs. Elle est évincée du commerce; il lui reste la propriété terrienne, dont elle ne sera pas la maîtresse exclusive. Sous l'ancien régime, elle se savait une élite; dorénavant, elle devra l'affirmer avec force...Ils [the members of the nobility] réclament des pensions, leur intégration dans l'armée britannique. L'Acte de Québec consacre leurs privilèges, protège juridiquement le régime de propriété sur lequel ils s'appuient. Plusieurs d'entre eux font partie du Conseil législatif.

The Church also had to conciliate and make concessions to the British. As a result it became one of the means by which the conquered were dominated by and remained, on the whole, at peace with their conquerors. Its role as an essential element of British policy is set out by Dumont (113).

> Après la Conquête, l'Église n'a pas de place désignée dans l'aménagement officiel de la métropole britannique: si le gouvernement anglais en préserve l'existence, ce n'est pas parce qu'il y voit, comme du temps de l'allégeance française, un rouage légitime d'une société; il la considère comme un inévitable moyen de domination de la population conquise.

Deprived of their natural leaders and insecure in their confidence in their political and legal rights, French people in Canada clung to their land and their religion, changing gradually from a society dominated by the adventurous *coureurs des bois* and *voyageurs* to one dominated by the *habitants*, who remained in their communities and cultivated their land, although the more adventurous did leave to undertake seasonal work in the lumber camps or to settle the new lands which were being opened up to the north and west in the nineteenth century. Whereas the *coureur de bois* needed space and freedom and chafed against the restrictions of living in a settled community, the *habitant* feared and avoided the idea of wilderness and clung to the familiar. The richer *habitants* could make use of seasonal workers to help them on the farms, and it is in these circumstances that the *survenants*, footloose and rootless young men, were to be found.[2] Moving wherever there was work and never settling permanently in any one place, they provided a reservoir of labour which usefully supplemented the local community at a period when agriculture was labour-intensive and physically very demanding.

The literary use of of such characters becomes really important only in the second part of the twentieth century with the novel, *Le Survenant*, which will be discussed in Chapter 3. In it Germaine Guèvremont looks at a year in the life of an agricultural community, still remote from Montréal, and the effect on it of the unexpected arrival of a survenant. The mindsets of the nomad and the settler are contrasted, as the one fears and shuns the restrictions of life in a community, while the other is not interested in and is frightened by the world outside the boundaries of the familiar. Lavoie argues in the conclusion to her article on the *coureur de bois* that the link between the survenant characters and the *coureurs de bois* is clear. Their longing for the wilderness continues the historical opposition between the two sections of society, the nomad and the settler. Unlike the *coureurs de bois*, however, the survenants have lost their *raison d'être* and with it their ability to act decisively. The contrast is made clear by Lavoie (25).

> Nous avons suffisamment montré, nous semble-t-il, ce rôle de l'espace dans la vie du coureur de bois, pour conclure que le héros de type Survenant est un héros aliéné, qui continue à opposer aux vertus de la durée, les prestiges de la conquête de l'espace, mais poursuit une course dérisoire sur une terre où il n'y a plus d'espace à conquérir. Fils spirituel du coureur de bois dont il ne diffère pas essentiellement, il est né dans un monde où nulle conquête n'est possible. Son errance n'est qu'une façon de se fuir lui-même pour échapper à l'insupportable conscience de son incapacité à transformer le monde.

The replacements of the *coureurs de bois* in the nineteenth and twentieth century did not have the same role as the men of earlier generations. As Lavoie shows, the memory of the *coureurs de bois* lingered, but the *quêteux* and the *survenants* who then make their appearance were different in many respects from their predecessors (21). Many of the *coureurs de bois* were of noble origin or ex-soldiers. When they had finished their adventurous life, they settled

---

[2] As survenant has no direct equivalent in English, I have used the term rather than try to find a substitute. Approximate equivalents are, amongst others, "newcomer", "outsider", "incomer" and "come-from-away".

down in their society to end their days surrounded by their own kind. The *quêteux*, however, begged for their living from door to door, depending on the ingrained tradition of alms-giving of strongly Christian communities. They had no roots in the communities which they visited, although they would reappear fairly regularly in the same places. They did not work for their living, and their contribution to the life of the community was to allow others to show their charity. Guèvremont, in her first published work, *En Pleine Terre*, a collection of short stories set in the Sorel region, which anticipates many of the themes of *Le Survenant*, shows that the *quêteux* were conscious of their worth. In her story *Un bon quêteux* (27-30) the angry *quêteux* leaves the house of the Beauchemin in a rage when he feels that he has not been given an adequate helping of bread. The *quêteux* did not see their role as humble or inferior. If they were not treated with the respect which they felt they deserved, they would retaliate, as the following scene shows (29-30).

> Debout de tout son long, le quêteux, outragé, toisa tous les Beauchemin. Ce n'était pas pour la valeur des choses qu'il s'indignait, lui l'homme libre d'aller de maison en maison où l'on se ferait fête de lui donner davantage, mais pour l'offense qu'il ressentait jusque dans la moelle des os. Les Beauchemin, inquiets, suivaient le moindre de ses gestes. Allait-il se changer en jeteux de sort? Dédaigneusement 'le grand quêteux d'étoffe' prit l'offrande et la laissa tomber sur la table. Puis, fièrement, rechargeant le baluchon à son dos, il les flagella de toute sa grandeur;
> - Vous vous en chercherez un bon quêteux comme moi.

The *survenants* were different. Like the *quêteux* they had no roots in a particular community, where they would reside for a short time before moving on to somewhere else. Unlike the *quêteux* they worked for their living and earned their bed and board, wherever there was a call for casual labour and not too many questions would be asked. As such they belong to the period when there was a heavy demand for casual labour, before agriculture had been mechanised. It was a period when physical strength was of prime importance. The type will forever be identified with Guèvremont's eponymous hero in her second book which is set in the years before the First World War. The author was just old enough to recall at first hand that period, when she was a teenager. The rural way of life would still have been familiar to the people of Sorel amongst whom she lived and worked in the 1930s. As conceived by Guèvremont the character of the Survenant is part of a rural setting which, although much cherished by traditionalists, was becoming part of Quebec's past, even as she wrote.

The Idea of the Survenant

The establishment of the survenant as a literary type under that name dates from 1945 when Guèvremont introduced her now famous character to the reading public. As the following chapters will show, her successors adopted the theme with enthusiasm, no doubt in part because of its Canadian resonances and also because of the opportunities created to analyse the conflicts and tensions caused by the arrival of a stranger within a settled community. Five major novels, generally accepted as classic works of Quebec literature, will illustrate the vitality of the theme in the second half of the twentieth century. Each novel shows how its author has adapted the theme to his or her needs and succeeded in illuminating a new area of conflict or tension within Quebec society.

Although the survenant belongs to a particular period of Quebec society, the idea of the disruptive stranger is not, of course, unique to French-Canadian literature. The incomer who has a profound effect on the community which he or she visits is found in folk-tale and literature throughout the ages and in many cultures. In the twentieth century it became an important theme in film in, for example, the Western with films like *High Noon* and *Bad Day at Black Rock*.

Anne Hébert in *Les Fous de Bassan* (1982) is clearly aware of such links with the wider theme. Her hero returns to his village, filled with resentment against his unloving mother and tempted to ingratiate himself with his grandmother, now the matriarch of the village. The parallels with Œdipus and Orestes are clear. Hébert makes the theme her own by changing the murder victims to the girl cousins of the incomer instead of his mother, but it is clear that they are actually the substitutes for her. His hatred of women is inspired by his sense of rejection by his mother, and he is haunted by memories of her coldness and the violence of his father. Hébert also explicitly links her tale to that of the Pied Piper of Hamelin by making her hero dream of escaping with his siblings from the harshness of their home. Again she introduces a variant on the original, as, unlike the parents of Hamelin, these parents would not regret the departure of their children.

Guèvremont does not openly link her tale to any antecedent, but her Survenant is not unlike Æneas. Handsome and virile, he arrives unexpectedly, as Æneas did in Carthage, and proceeds to win the love of one of the ladies in the village. Unlike Æneas and Dido, the

Survenant and Angélina do not become lovers, but it is generally accepted that he is her suitor, and it is obvious to all who have eyes to see that she is desperately in love with him. Like Æneas, the Survenant slips away secretly leaving his beloved behind and, like Dido, Angélina is inconsolable, although she does not go so far as to commit suicide.

Gilles Deschênes in Louis Hamelin's *Cowboy* (1992) has points in common with another classical hero, Jason. Like Jason, he travels to a remote community, which is in his case a village close to an Indian reserve in the north of the province. While there, he has affairs with two of the women, one white, one Indian, causing considerable tension in both communities. Also like Jason, he has a base, Montreal, to return to, leaving behind him the chaos and the distress to which he has contributed.

In *Le Libraire* (1960) Bessette's hero, Jodoin, is multi-faceted. He turns out to be a thief as well as a humorist and so can be linked to the trickster, the figure of folk-tale and myth found in most cultures. Skilfully he deceives those who would try to deceive him. Parallels with certain aspects of his behaviour can therefore be drawn with Prometheus, who stole fire from the Greek gods, or with Coyote on the North American continent and Till Eulenspiegel in Europe. There are many stories about the latter two outwitting their opponents and causing havoc in the communities which they visit. One of the main differences between Jodoin and Prometheus or Till is that, unlike them, he does not suffer for his trickery, but withdraws to enjoy his profits in a life of comparative ease in Montreal.

Langevin's Alain Dubois in *Poussière sur la ville* (1952) is the only one of the five for whom there is no obvious classical parallel. Ridden with angst and uncertainty, he is very much a man of the twentieth century, whose like is to be found in the writing of Sartre and Camus. Characters like Sartre's Roquentin or Camus's Dr. Rieux have much in common with Dubois. Langevin uses the theme of the survenant to probe the anguish of a man who sees himself failing at everything that matters to him. His hero is a survenant who is completely different from the other four under discussion, as he is rendered impotent by his failure to see how others see him or to appreciate how his actions are interpreted.

Other francophone Canadian authors have used the same theme, and indeed some of the authors already mentioned have used it in other books. Anne Hébert uses variations of it in both *Kamouraska* and *Les Enfants du Sabbat*. In the former, Dr. George Nelson, the lover of the heroine Elisabeth Rolland, is in every way an outsider in the community of Sorel where he has settled after the flight of his Loyalist family from the United States. With his anglophone and protestant background and his medical knowledge which is far in advance of the beliefs of the people, Dr. Nelson is seen as suspect, and his affair with Elisabeth causes a scandal. Ultimately he has to flee to Vermont after murdering Elisabeth's husband and disappears from her life to resume his status as an outsider, this time as a fugitive criminal as well as the son of a former rebel and émigré. In *Les Enfants du Sabbat* Soeur Julie, the child of sorcerers, causes havoc in the religious community where she has sought shelter and which she eventually leaves to disappear mysteriously with her demonic lover. A satanist and devil worshipper, Soeur Julie is a survenante of the most evil and destructive kind.

In *Miss Charlie* Suzanne Paradis makes her survenant a wealthy American writer who destroys the peace of mind of a young widow and her niece when he takes the house next door to theirs. When he leaves to return to New York, he leaves behind him a scene of devastation literally and figuratively. Like most of the other survenants, he himself seems unscathed and uncaring. Suzanne Jacob's *Laura Laur* has a survenante, a young, rootless girl who brings unhappiness and confusion to the businessman who gets involved with her. Louis Lefebvre in *Guanahani* makes his survenant the narrator in an historical novel set in the time of Christopher Columbus who takes back to Spain the son of a Carib chief. Intelligent and sceptical, the young Carib could see the weaknesses of his own culture which succumbed so rapidly to the invading Europeans, but once in Spain this outsider looks critically at European society, gradually understanding more and more of the corruption and violence behind the sophisticated mask of Spanish society. Thus Lefebvre gives a new twist to the theme by which the conquered are empowered to assess and criticise the conquerors. Antonine Maillet also uses an historical setting in *Crache à pic* where the customs officer, sent to the Maritimes to put an end to the bootlegging of the Prohibition Era, changes the life of the eponymous heroine and then, by his death, ruins the ambitions of the local crime chief.

None of the authors mentioned above use the same setting as Guèvremont, who established the theme as an important one in Quebec. She was chronicling a disappearing way of life, so that it is no surprise that her successors in Quebec literature rarely adopt the same agricultural setting, which, as Robert Baillie reminds us, would flourish for the last time in the writings of Guèvremont (21). '*Le Survenant* constitue le dernier témoignage de ce qu'il est coutume d'appeler au Québec le roman de tradition rurale.' At almost the same time Gabrielle Roy published her most famous book, *Bonheur d'occasion*, one of whose themes is the increasing urbanisation of Quebec. Roy studies the lives of first-generation rural emigrants in Montreal whose links with the countryside of their birth are fading fast. André Langevin also chooses an urban setting for *Poussière sur la ville*. The theme of the survenant survives, but the survenants of the second half of the twentieth century are town dwellers and may well be bourgeois intellectuals rather than manual labourers. This is one of the reasons for including a study of Bessette's *Le Libraire*, which forms a bridge between Guèvremont and later novelists. The estrangement of such intellectuals from the community which they are visiting can stem from differences in class and education which give them a more liberal, less traditional outlook on life. In this respect, of course, they are not so different from Guèvremont's Survenant and are just as dangerous as he was.

Le Survenant; Germaine Guèvremont

Germaine Guèvremont published *Le Survenant* in 1945. The success of this novel and its sequel, *Marie-Didace*, in 1947, coupled with the popularity of the radio serial based on the novels, which was transmitted in the early fifties and again in the sixties, made the concept of the survenant familiar to a wide audience in Quebec. James J. Herlan has studied the radio series (38).

> The original radio version of *Le Survenant* began on 31 August 1953, and continued until 6 May 1955. There were five broadcasts a week, Monday through Friday, with each episode lasting fifteen minutes. The popularity of the program can be assumed, since the original series was rebroadcast from the autumn of 1962 to the spring of 1965.

The novel quickly became known to an international audience through the success of the translations which appeared very early after the initial publication of the novels (*The Outlander*. Translated by Eric Sutton, Toronto: McGraw Hill of Canada Limited, 1950. *Monk's Reach*, London: Evans Bros., 1950. [Both translations include *Marie-Didace*]). Guèvremont saw herself as writing a 'roman de la paroisse', a term she used in an unpublished lecture (Germaine Guèvremont, "Les petites joies d'un grand métier" texte dactylographié, [1945], 19f., Archives nationales du Québec à Sherbrooke, fonds Alfred DesRochers), which is quoted by Lepage (164).

> Louis Hémon et Claude-Henri Grignon avaient écrit le roman du colon, Léo-Paul Desrosiers, le roman de la traite, Ringuet, le roman des déracinés, il restait encore celui de la vieille paroisse canadienne. De plus en plus se dessinait dans mon esprit la vieille paroisse que je n'avais fait qu'esquisser dans *En pleine terre*...

She did not use the terms 'roman régionaliste' or 'roman du terroir' which were the categories into which her books were slotted by some critics such as Lepage, who sees her book as coming at the end of the tradition of the *roman du terroir* and conforming, in part, to the models of that tradition, but, at the same time, shattering the closed world of those who worked the land by introducing a charismatic hero preaching the freedom and irresponsibility of youth (1998, 8). As Pierre Girouard has said, her characters are not like the characters of Ringuet in *Trente Arpents* and are not dominated by the land to the exclusion of all else (22-23). They have time for hunting and a limited degree of recreation within their own narrow circle. The author is much more interested in their emotional and social development than in the actual work on the land. They are, however, typical of their class and generation in that their horizons are limited to a very small geographical area, and they are suspicious of any incomer, even of one from only a few villages away. Guèvremont saw her book as partly about the difference between the two traditions in the history of the people of Québec, the tradition of the *coureur de bois* and the tradition of the *habitant*, as she made clear in her interview with Alice Parizeau in 1968 (12-15) which is quoted by Jean-Pierre Duquette (14).

> La société, notre société, se compose de deux races fondamentales. D'une part il y a des "habitants" qui sont des gens solides ayant les deux pieds sur la terre et, d'autre part, il y a les "coureurs de bois", les aventuriers, les meneurs.

As Gilles Marcotte demonstrated in *Une littérature qui se fait*, she differs from her predecessors in that she did not use her novel to give voice to nationalist politics or to develop a theory of land tenure (37).

> La romancière du *Survenant* a été la première, au Canada français, à dessiner un paysage terrien qui ne soit pas la projection d'un rêve nationaliste, ou d'un rêve de possession, mais un paysage humain et le lieu d'une existence possible.

Instead she concentrated on the human characteristics of the inhabitants of a small community in rural Quebec who are neither poverty-stricken nor colonising unsettled territory. Rather they are well established on land farmed by their ancestors for five or six generations and, for the most part, not dissatisfied with their life which has changed little from that of their ancestors.

Into this closed community one autumn evening comes a young, handsome stranger who stops at the farm of the Beauchemin family with whom he agrees to work as a farm hand in return for board and lodging. As he does not reveal his name or his background, the patriarch, Didace, calls him the Survenant, and thereafter he is known throughout the community by that name. Although the Survenant is welcomed by Didace who respects his aggressive spirit and his refusal to be cowed in the face of Didace's own aggression, Didace's son, Amable, and his daughter-in-law, Alphonsine, are far less welcoming to the intruder who is, in their eyes, a threat to their peaceful existence. In fact, their suspicions are justified, as the Survenant quickly proves to be an unsettling element not only in the Beauchemin family but in the whole community of Chenal du Moine. André Vanasse links this reaction to the history of the French-Canadians, a race which had been defeated and therefore resents those whose courage and energy underline their state of submission (609).

> On comprend donc les sentiments ambivalents qui entourent l'Étranger. Admiration parce que la société retrouve en lui l'énergie et le courage qu'elle voudrait avoir; haine parce qu'elle constate que sa condition historique l'oblige à vivre dans la soumission.

Neighbours divide between those like Didace and Angélina, the daughter of his neighbour, David Desmarais, who are drawn to the Survenant, and those like Amable and Pierre-Côme Provençal, the local *maire*, who detest him, so that, as Robidoux and Renard suggest, his arrival brings into the open all the underlying tensions of the community (56).

> L'arrivée du Survenant déclenche tous les conflits: une intrigue amoureuse, un drame conjugal, un problème de lignage etc.

The Survenant sees at first glance that the Beauchemin farm is not as well-tended as it ought to be. Despite its appearance of wealth and solidity it has lacked attention and maintenance recently. Didace has been disheartened by the deaths in quick succession of his promising younger son, Ephrem, his wife, Mathilde and his mother, *l'aïeule*. Since the death of his wife the house has lacked comfort, as Alphonsine, for all her good intentions, is too frail to be a good housewife and is not capable of the physical effort necessary. Amable is also weak and easily discouraged so that there is no-one to support Didace who shuns the house of too many memories and neglects the farm work for the pleasures of duck-shooting to which he has always been addicted. The watery landscape of the Chenal du Moine is not ideal for agriculture, so that it is no surprise that its inhabitants prefer to escape to the more agreeable pastimes of fishing and shooting

(Lepage, 1998, 63). The arrival of the Survenant changes that. Strong and willing to work, he can outperform even Didace and throws himself into the work around the farm so effectively that Alphonsine admits to Angélina that his arrival has made a great difference. She is already prepared for winter.

> - On a déjà quasiment tout notre hivernement. Pour dire la vérité, depuis son arrivée, le Survenant a fait donner une vraie bourrée à mes hommes...(29)

Didace rejoices in the physical strength and energy of the Survenant in whom he sees himself reborn and with whom, as Mireille Servais-Maquoi shows, he rapidly forges a close bond (206).

> La farouche énergie que déploie l'étranger au travail des champs, exacte antithèse de la faiblesse physique d'Amable, tisse peu à peu entre lui et le père Didace des liens solides d'affection.

Gradually the Survenant comes to assume the place of the son he does not have. The Survenant has the qualities and the defects that Didace had himself as a young man - a hard worker, a hard drinker and a great fighter, afraid of nothing and no one. With his arrival Didace begins to recapture some *joie de vivre*. Paul-Emile Roy argues that, for a moment, Didace is rejuvenated (33).

> La présence du Survenant réveille en Didace une vitalité endormie, elle lui redonne un instant toute l'ardeur de sa jeunesse.

They go drinking together in the taverns of Sorel and perhaps whoring, although that is not stated specifically. Didace refuses to join in the condemnation of the Survenant's drinking which he seems to accept with equanimity. For Jean Morency the drinking of the Survenant is an essential part of his personality which disturbs and unsettles any community to which he temporarily attaches himself and to which he inevitably brings the carnival atmosphere associated with alcohol (74).

> ...le roman de Germaine Guèvremont accorde une place centrale à la figure de Dionysos, pour en faire, sous les traits du Survenant, une sorte d'anti-héros, assez représentatif lui aussi de la tradition littéraire états-unienne...Cette vision [du Survenant] est celle du nomade, du vagabond, du *gipsy*, qui parcourt le continent sans jamais pouvoir se fixer quelque part, dans un tourbillon et une fête perpétuels, qui forment une sorte de

bacchanale ininterrompue, que vient souligner la relation privilégiée qui existe entre le personnage et la dive bouteille.

The *fête perpétuelle* is perhaps an exaggeration, but the close and frequent relationship between the Survenant and the bottle is there for all to see.

When sober, which he is for most of the time as he is a binge drinker rather than a perpetual drunkard, the Survenant is an exemplary worker. The farm work progresses more easily when Didace and the Survenant work together. Amable is quite incapable of matching their work rate, collapsing with nose bleeds and fatigue. When the Survenant turns out be an inexpert hunter, Didace shows him how to hunt for muskrats and is mightily impressed by the Survenant's knowledge of carpentry. His affection for the Survenant is such that he does not even react when the Survenant spends all the profits from the carpentry on a prolonged drinking session in Sorel, wasting the money which Didace had given him to spend on new tools in Montreal. Their closeness comes out during the voyage in the canoe which the Survenant has constructed for Didace, when they discover that it is possible that they are related as both have ancestors with the surname Petit. As Ducrocq-Poirier points out Didace is intimidated a little by the superior knowledge of the Survenant (335). '...le père Didace se sent "dominé" par l'instruction de son engagé.' The result is that he does not pursue the connection while the Survenant lets the subject drop as being of little interest. Nonetheless during this voyage and also during the fight between the Survenant amd Odilon Provençal, Didace feels great closeness to the Survenant who, as Baillie suggests, is replacing the weakling son in the affections of the older man (85). 'Le rôle du fils est assumé par l'étranger qui supplée aux carences du sang déchu.' As he watches the brutal struggle between the two younger men, Didace is carried back in time to his own fighting days. At the end he is filled with pride at the outcome.

> Didace ne l'entendit même pas. Une grosse joie bouillonnait en lui avec son sang redevenu riche et ardent. Sa face terreuse sillonnée par l'âge, ses forces en déclin, son vieux coeur labouré d'inquiétude? Un mauvais rêve. Il retrouvait sa jeune force intacte: Didace, fils de Didace, vient de prendre possession de la terre. Il a trente ans. Un premier fils lui est né. Le règne des Beauchemin n'aura jamais de fin.
>
> C'était lui qui se battait à la place du Survenant. Ses muscles durcissaient sous l'effort. L'écume à la bouche et la tête au guet, les jambes écartées et les bras en ciseaux. Il affrontait l'adversaire. V'lan

dans le coffre! Ses poings, deux masses de fer, cognaient dur, fouillaient les flancs de l'autre. Les coups qu'il aurait portés, le Survenant les portait. Vise en plein dans les côtés. Tu l'as! (97-98)

The new surge of energy which Didace feels as a result of the presence of the Survenant is coupled with the great respect he feels for the judgement of the Survenant. Didace is aged about sixty, and it is clear from the way that he refers to his father who was still working in the fields at fifty-five that this was considered a good age for a man. Didace accepted his status as an ageing widower, until the Survenant puts into his head the idea that he might remarry and raise a couple of vigorous sons to continue the line which Amable seems unlikely to do. Alphonsine is still childless after three years of marriage.

> Vous êtes loin d'être vieux. Vous pourriez encore élever une famille....
> Inconsciemment Didace redressa ses épaules affaissées.
> - On le sait ben; j'suis pas des plus jeunes, mais j'suis pas vieux, vieux comme il y en a, pour mon temps. (142)

The Survenant, who, according to Alain Charbonneau, provides considerable erotic force in the book (68-70), also introduces the name of the Acayenne, another outsider, as a possible bride for Didace. At the end, after the Survenant has left the farm for ever, Didace, still under the invigorating influence of the Survenant, as Major suggests, decides to marry the Acayenne immediately (197).

> ...le Survenant insufflant en lui des énergies qu'il croyait épuisés depuis longtemps et auxquelles il ne songeait même plus, telles cette vigueur sexuelle et cette capacité de procréation, manifestations par excellence de l'érotisme, qui encouragent Didace à se remarier.

He will not wait for the priest to contact her parish of origin to find out about her. His confidence in the judgement of the Survenant is such that he has, in effect, allowed the Survenant to choose his bride for him. In this way the influence of the Survenant lives on after his departure. In *Marie-Didace* l'Acayenne arrives in Chenal du Moine and is installed as the wife of Didace, immediately displacing Alphonsine. Her role is, in many ways, parallel to that of the Survenant in the first volume as she is the driving force in the novel, forcing the other characters to react to her presence, as Rita Leclerc has said (65). 'Elle [l'Acayenne] joue, dans ce roman, le rôle dévolu au Survenant dans le précédent; le rôle de catalyseur, pivot de l'intrigue.'

The other male character most obviously influenced by the Survenant is Joinville Provençal, the youngest son of Pierre-Côme. Like his brothers he is teetotal and very much under the influence of his father who detests the Survenant from his first meeting with him. Indeed he goes out of his way to warn Joinville against the influence of the Survenant, to whom he attributes Indian blood, which in the eyes of the *habitants* was both a disgrace and a cause for suspicion. Joinville protests that the colouring of the Survenant is all wrong for an Indian, but Pierre-Côme retorts that the Survenant never smiles which is typical of Indians, a reaction which Vanasse sees as typical of his kind, as the resident population is always hostile to the nomad or the gypsy (39).

> Élément majoritaire de la population, le sédentaire s'acharnera sur le nomade, mais il lui faut, pour se donner bonne conscience, lui attribuer une origine qui le distingue essentiellement de la sienne propre. L'étranger deviendra, bien souvent malgré lui, un Indien.

While his eldest son, Odilon, joins in his father's loathing of the Survenant, Joinville falls completely under his influence during the visit of the circus to Sorel. The Survenant gains immense prestige among the men of Chenal du Moine by winning a bout against a professional wrestler in the fairground booth. After his victory they all depart to the inn to drink to his success, but when the money runs out, the Survenant manœuvres Joinville into using his profits from the day's trading in the market to finance the next round of drinking. The next day Angélina is horrified to discover Joinville dead drunk in a ditch not far from her house, wearing the lumberjacket of the Survenant. As a result the Provençal are only too delighted when the Survenant disappears, as they will never forgive what he has done to two of their sons. Whereas the defeat of Odilon had no lasting effect on him beyond increasing his dislike of the Survenant, Joinville never recovers from his introduction to drink. In *Marie-Didace* he has escaped from his father by working in Sorel during the war, but he has acquired the habit of drinking too much. Didace sees him walking past one day, drunk, his shirt undone in the way the Survenant used to wear his. Didace is not impressed. In his opinion Joinville can be only a poor imitation of the Survenant as he lacks the qualities of the man himself.

The Survenant's drinking does not deter Angélina Desmarais, the old maid, who has rejected all the eligible bachelors in the district. From the first sight of him she is attracted by his personality and his physical presence, and she is not alone in this, as Major points out (46).

> Même la lecture la plus sommaire du roman fait apparaître la fascination proprement érotique que le Survenant exerce sur les personnages masculins autant que féminins.

The Survenant is extremely attractive to the women of Chenal du Moine, perhaps in part because he is so different from the men to whom they are accustomed. He is tall, rangy, well-built with fiery red hair and a delicate white skin. As Richard Williamson points out, Angélina is drawn to him first of all by his physical attractiveness (248). '...the Survenant exudes a strong, sexual attraction through two physical characteristics noticed first by Angélina, his hands and his fiery red hair.' Some of the women are also piqued by his obvious lack of interest in them, but, even so, it seems unlikely that the theory of Adrien Thério – that the Survenant is a homosexual – is correct (25-28). In *Marie-Didace* the Acayenne takes pleasure in pointing out to the girls of Chenal du Moine that the Survenant had not always been indifferent to girls (64-65).

> Allez pas vous inventionner de croire qu'il avait jamais rencontré de filles avant d'arriver au Chenal du Moine, le Survenant. Il en connaissait, de quoi en saler! Des créatures de toutes les sortes.

Her words suggest a heterosexual, if licentious, lifestyle, so that, although Thério is no doubt right to argue that the moral climate of the 1940s would have made it difficult for Guèvremont to make one of her characters openly homosexual, it seems probable that the question did not arise for her. He cannot tell the four Provençal girls apart and pays so little attention to the women that he can confuse Rose-de-Lima Bibeau, the extremely plain schoolteacher, with the reigning beauty of the area, Bernadette Salvail. He is aware that Angélina is attracted to him, however, and gradually he responds to her obvious admiration. His fight with Odilon is partly provoked by the latter's contempt for Angélina, who has rejected him, and partly by Odilon's sneers about l'Acayenne. After that it is accepted by everyone that the Survenant is Angélina's champion, and she is left alone.

Under the influence of her love for him Angélina blossoms, recovering some of her attractiveness which had been fading as she aged and, as Major suggests, gaining in confidence and recapturing some of the bloom of youth (198).

> L'amour se manifeste chez elle [Angélina], comme la contemplation narcissique chez Didace, par une espèce de renaissance et un acte de confiance à la vie.

Because she is in love, she will overlook his drinking. She will find excuses for his behaviour. When he gives her some sweets in a parcel whose wrapping is half-undone as an Easter present as she comes out of mass, she forgives him his cruel behaviour of the day before. He had left her in Sorel to wait for him and gone drinking instead of coming to the meeting point, where she was left stranded, an object of curiosity or derision to the onlookers. She cannot stay away from the Beauchemin house when she thinks that he will be there. When she suspects that he is preparing to leave and return to the road, she offers everything that she can think of to keep him by her. She will change her harmonium for a piano. She will pay for new clothes. She even goes so far as to offer herself and her inheritance to him. Nothing that she can do will tempt him. Angélina and the Survenant symbolise the clash of the nomad and the settler; if Angélina had persuaded him to stay, her success would undoubtedly have been fatal to their love. The Survenant knows that it would be cruel to accept the offer of Angélina, and so he leaves without explaining. After his departure, Angélina, who has already made so many sacrifices for the Survenant, nerves herself to go round and settle all his debts, so that, whatever the gossip about her, his name will be clear. Then she gives way to a grief from which even Marie-Amanda, the daughter of Didace, has difficulty in rousing her. Angélina makes no bones about the fact that she would have given the Survenant anything that he wanted. She would even have taken to the road with him, but Marie-Amanda manages to show her that whatever she had done, in the end she would have lost him. Angélina has had one year of happiness and must be content with that, because, as Suzanne Paradis argues, she has gained emotionally from his presence (42).

> Le passage du Survenant a rajeuni et mûri à la fois Angélina. Il lui a permis de donner des dimensions nouvelles au petit bonheur qu'elle possédait déjà; il ne lui apportait pas ce bonheur entièrement neuf, inhabité encore, d'un partage total, égal.

In *Marie-Didace* she is still faithful to his memory, but years later she is shown an old newspaper photograph of a dead war hero whom she recognises as the Survenant. She alone identifies it, but at last she knows that he will never return, which had been her secret hope. Even though she had never actually married him, she considers herself his widow, which gives her courage and confidence.

> Et elle se sentit veuve. Un sentiment de fierté lui fit redresser la tête. Désormais, au lieu de l'humiliation de la vieille fille déjetée, elle porterait en sa personne la dignité d'une veuve. (204)

Before the arrival of the Survenant Angélina had led a quiet, peaceful life with her father. From the moment that she saw him, life would never be the same again, since, as Girouard says, he introduced her to the notion of love (39). 'Grâce au Survenant elle fait la découverte de la dimension érotique de l'existence.' Like Didace, Angélina found that the Survenant had completely changed the course of her life. As Robidoux and Renard point out (55), she is not alone in that.

> En un peu plus d'une année seulement, à cause de lui, tout change au Chenal du Moine; le rythme de l'existence se transforme et personne n'aura traversé intact la période du séjour de Venant.

Unlike Angélina, Alphonsine did not immediately succumb to the attraction of the Survenant. She was angered by the careless way he splashed water on the floor which gave her so much trouble to keep clean. She resented the way he used her cup and teased her, calling her 'la petite mère'. Like most of her class she had a horror of the dangers of alcohol which had ruined several farmers, but in her case the horror was greater, because she knew the part that alcohol had played in her own father's neglect of her. Gradually, however, she is won over by the Survenant. She realises the difference he makes to life in the Beauchemin household. In many ways her work is made easier because the Survenant does his share of the work promptly and efficiently. He has an eye for what needs to be done and does it without waiting to be told. The wood box is always full of just the right sort of wood. She is able to make good progress with her preparations for the winter and, as Baillie comments (49), she can even describe the results of his presence as 'une vraie bénédiction' (29). She is touched when he brings her a bundle of sweet grass which she can put amongst the clothes in the drawers of her chest to perfume them. The Beauchemin men never think of such gestures. She is attracted by his physical beauty and, longing for a child of her own, she treats him like one when he turns up drunk from Sorel. Lepage sees this episode as revealing both the gradual softening of Alphonsine as she moves from pity to affection and the pathos of the Survenant, who has hitherto hidden his weakness and loneliness but is now shown to be 'un grand enfant solitaire et fragile' (1998, 92). She would like to mother him and look after him, but the Survenant has no intention of allowing any woman that degree of control. His feelings are made clear when he rejects the offers of both Alphonsine and Angélina to sew the missing buttons on his shirt. Little by little Alphonsine accepts him as part of the household, a fact which Amable notes without enthusiasm. Her changing attitude adds to Amable's resentment of the stranger as he feels himself more and more isolated in his own home. His feelings are perceptively analysed by Lepage (1998, 158).

> Mais chaque fois que le Survenant se montre prévenant avec Alphonsine ou qu'il est de connivence avec le père Didace, Amable en éprouve dépit et amertume. Aussi se réjouit-il sans vergogne de son départ, qui constitue pour lui une véritable libération. L'étranger menaçait en effet d'usurper son double titre de fils et de mari: on comprend mieux ainsi pourquoi il déteste tellement celui en qui il ne voit qu'un rival.

The great change for Alphonsine during the stay of the Survenant is that she finally becomes pregnant. Although the Survenant is not physically responsible for this, his presence in the community has been a symbol of a renewal of life and energy. He has given Didace a new lease of life. He has awoken Angélina from her sterile spinsterhood, and Alphonsine responds to his vitality by creating new life, the future Marie-Didace, starting to fulfil the traditional woman's role of wife and mother. This idea is taken even further by Girouard and Major, the former arguing that it is thanks to the Survenant that she regains her feminine identity ('c'est lui qui l'a en quelque sorte "reféminisée"') (40-41), while the latter suggests that the Survenant is indirectly the father of Alphonsine's child (201). '...le Survenant, source de vie, force vitale, est le véritable père spirituel de l'enfant qu'Alphonsine porte et le grand responsible de sa grossesse.' Such a claim seems hard on Amable who is undoubtedly the physical father, as Didace will eventually be delighted to recognise Beauchemin features in Marie-Didace which can come only from Amable. Although Alphonsine joins Amable in his criticisms of the Survenant after his departure, when, in *Marie-Didace*, she thinks that he has returned a few days later, Amable is quick to hear the note of joy in her voice and reacts with bitter jealousy (14). The effect of the Survenant on the young couple is every bit as great as on Didace. Thanks to him Didace has remarried and introduced into their house a survenante, the Acayenne. The older, more capable woman quickly replaces Alphonsine as the principal housewife, usurping the place which it had been Alphonsine's ambition to fill. Patricia Smart comments on the inevitability of change following the remarriage (115).

> Not only a non-Quebecois, but a woman who dares to make her presence felt in the house, she necessarily upsets the existing order of things.

Her arrival fills Alphonsine with fear that she and Amable will be disinherited to the advantage of this woman and her stepson, and she nags Amable to assert himself with his father to secure his inheritance. Her efforts are useless. Didace will not be intimidated by a son he despises, and when Amable overhears the Acayenne insinuating that Alphonsine was in love with the Survenant, he quarrels with his father. Soon afterwards Alphonsine persuades him to leave the house to force his father to accept his terms. This plan too is a failure. Amable is killed in an industrial accident in the docks at Montreal. No doubt he had sought work there after hearing the Survenant talk romantically about the work of a docker. Alphonsine can bitterly reflect that, if the Survenant had never come to Chenal du Moine, life for her, Amable and Didace would have continued in its peaceful routine.

> Le Survenant n'avait pas porté bonheur aux Beauchemin. Vrai, sa puissance magnétique n'avait plus guère de reflet sur eux; mais le sillon de malheur qu'il avait creusé inconsciemment autour de leur maison, six ans plus tard le temps ne l'avait pas encore comblé. Cette femme, l'Acayenne, elle n'était pas des leurs, elle les frustrait d'une part du vieux bien et sans cesse elle les menaçait de la présence du fils de son Varieur, cette femme, qui prenait toujours la part de Marie-Didace et qui se faisait aimer de l'enfant au détriment de Phonsine, c'était le Survenant qui l'avait présentée au père Didace. Sans elle, sans son œuvre sournoise, Amable n'aurait jamais quitté le Chenal du Moine, et il ne serait pas mort. Chaque nuit, Phonsine ne retrouverait pas la sombre hantise de voir sa petite tomber dans le puits. (*M-D*, 166)

Instead their life was completely overturned. During the stay of the Survenant the fortunes of the Beauchemin knew a brief upturn, but after his departure the arrival of the Acayenne brought nothing but trouble, quarrels and disappointment. Whereas the Survenant had the gift of giving, the Survenante had not. Instead she took for herself, and Didace comes to realise quite quickly that she is no replacement for Mathilde. Where Mathilde, like his mother and sisters and the indomitable Marie-Amanda, had the gift of bringing life to a house and its inhabitants, the Acayenne, for all her technical expertise, cannot do that. The Survenant could fill the house with warmth and life, temporarily replacing the dead Mathilde. Robert Major argues, however, that the Acayenne neither has, nor desires to have, this skill (206).

> En somme, cette femme [l'Acayenne] ressemble en tous points au Survenant. Mais elle n'en a que les apparences...L'Acayenne est une fausse 'survenante', ou plutôt une 'survenante' sans l'essentiel, le don de la vie.

She brings with her disharmony and suspicion, bitterness and greed. As Patricia Smart shows, she never integrates into the world of Chenal du Moine, for her thoughts are constantly far away with her own people and the water where she has spent much of her life (116).

The other female character who is affected by the Survenant is the beautiful Bernadette Salvail. Accustomed to the admiration of the young men, she expects to add the Survenant to her court. His lack of interest both attracts and infuriates her. At the party thrown by the Salvail she tries to persuade him to sing, but he will only do so if she gives him a drink. She plays for time by promising the drink after he has sung, but he is adamant. She has to give way and takes him to her father's brandy. She watches him fill the glass four times and drain it, oblivious of her presence. Together with the reader she realises that drinking is the Survenant's true love, as Allard suggests (1997, 60-61).

> Le lecteur découvrira avec la Bernadette que l'amour et les caresses de l'homme vont exclusivement au caribou, à l'alcool...un amour passionné mais dévié, justement, vers un plaisir solitaire.

She realises that she cannot compete with his passion for alcohol.

Une brume se levait entre Bernadette et lui. Ils étaient à la fois ensemble et séparés. "Quel safre!" pensa-t-elle, indignée de le voir emplir son verre une quatrième fois. Mais en même temps elle éprouvait de la gêne et de la honte et aussi l'ombre d'un regret inavoué: le sentiment pénible d'être témoin d'une extase à laquelle elle ne participait point. (93)

Bernadette is not pleased that Angélina can attract the Survenant when she cannot. She had specifically invited him to the party. Even after her eyes are opened by the episode with the brandy, she is jealous of Angélina and will make spiteful remarks about her behaviour. Nonetheless she no longer finds the Survenant so attractive that she will make a real effort to interest him. She takes the hint when Angélina makes it clear that she is unwelcome when the Survenant is playing the harmonium. After she has amused herself by interrupting Angélina's pleasant dream, she leaves. She has not entirely lost interest in the Survenant but she is not prepared to waste her time on someone who is so clearly uninterested in her. Bernadette suffers less than the others from the arrival of the Survenant, but his lack of interest in her teaches her the limit of her power.

While the principal characters all find their lives changed by the arrival and the departure of the Survenant, he also has an effect on the whole community, as Duquette points out (5).

...le passage du Survenant bouleverse tout et vient signifier comme une rupture à tous les niveaux du texte.

The people of Chenal du Moine are intensely parochial. Apart from a few restless young men like Ludger Aubuchon, the husband of Marie-Amanda, who sign on as sailors and go voyaging down the Saint-Lawrence, the majority of the inhabitants stay where they were born. Pierre-Côme typifies the local patriotism, their pride in their identity and their suspicion of anyone who is a stranger, especially someone who can trounce one of their own sons.

Sauf Pierre-Côme Provençal, vexé dans son orgueil de voir un de la paroisse, à plus forte raison son fils, recevoir une rincée aux mains d'un étranger qu'il tenait pour un larron, par le fait même qu'il ignorait tout de lui. (98)

Baillie sees the fight between the two young men as a conflict between the two clans and suggests that it leaves the community more deeply divided. He notes that, unlike Didace and Pierre-Côme, who shook hands after their battles, Odilon and the Survenant do not shake hands, indicating that the ill-feeling persists (91-92). Nonetheless the Survenant is the centre of attention from the moment of his arrival at the Beauchemin house. Girouard sees him to be both the principal character and the dynamic element in the plot (28).

> Le Survenant, personnage central, est le conducteur de l'intrigue, c'est lui qui met le drame en place, qui est au coeur des préoccupations et qui fascine tous les autres...

The neighbours come to spend the evenings there to be entertained by the tales he has to tell. Didace no longer shuns his home but instead is happy to spend his time with the circle of his friends and acquaintances in his own kitchen. The house recovers the life and warmth that it had while his wife, Mathilde, was alive. The arrival of the Survenant offers the villagers a glimpse of the world outside which simultaneously fascinates and repels them.

For the inhabitants of Chenal du Moine what counts is the land. Didace has an intense pride in being the sixth Didace, son of Didace, and his dearest wish is to be able to hand his land on to a worthy successor. He envies Pierre-Côme with his four strapping sons and his four daughters, all attached to the community like their father. There is a huge gulf between his attitude and that of the Survenant with his longing for the open road, his reluctance to accept any ties and his lack of interest in acquiring any possessions. As Lepage has argued, the difference between the two men is symbolised by the story of the two Beauchemin brothers, who may be their ancestors (1998, 95). The conversation which takes place between the Survenant and Didace when they are together in Didace's canoe brings out this ambivalence in the French-Canadian male. Didace relates the story of his own ancestors, two brothers, who came from France to seek their fortune and arrived one winter in the Chenal du Moine to work in the lumber camps, intending to depart in the spring. During the winter the elder brother fell in love with *une créature* and did not return to the road in the spring, when the younger left alone. Thus in the same family the instinct of the *habitant* and the *coureur de bois* or *quêteux* are found side by side. This is the point at which Guèvremont hints at a possible relationship between the two men who would typify two strands in French-Canadian history, the settler and the adventurer. (Girouard argues that there are in fact three different categories (31). '...le coureur de bois, sauvage et enclin à la boisson, affirmant des valeurs de liberté et des attitudes de libertinage; ensuite le quêteux, personnage mystérieux, presque charlatan et jeteux de sort en puissance; et enfin l'engagé, ce bon travaillant habile de ses mains et possédant une vaste expérience de toutes les besognes...' There is no example of a *quêteux* in *Le Survenant*, although there is a *quêteux* in one of the stories in *En pleine terre*.) The possibility of their kinship is picked up again in *Marie-Didace* when Angélina shows the photograph of the Survenant to the shopkeeper who cannot identify it but thinks that it has a look of père Didace when young. The conversation between the two men in the canoe dies away but Didace is confident that soon the Survenant will marry Angélina and daydreams that one day he will be more powerful than Pierre-Côme. He has misjudged his man, however, for the Survenant is the younger brother, not the elder, and will never succumb to the attractions of *une créature*, not even one as undemanding and devoted as Angélina. Her wealth has no interest for him, and he quickly gets impatient of the parochialism and narrow-mindedness of the people of Chenal du Moine. As Lepage says, the Survenant is a free spirit (1998, 125-6).

> Libre de toute entrave, doué de multiples qualités, le Survenant incarne les valeurs modernes que sont la curiosité, l'ouverture et la disponibilité d'esprit.

The farmers of Chenal du Moine cannot enter into his excitement at the idea of the open road, and they have no desire whatever to experience the uncertainty of his way of life. Ducrocq-Poirier accurately states that there is no real contact between the Survenant and the rest of the community (341).

> Pas une fois une réelle communication ne s'ouvre entre lui et les autres, pas une fois il ne se sent solidaire d'eux et fraternel à leur égard.

He is, in fact, as Servais-Maquoi points out, a sharp critic of the *habitants* with their dull and limited routines '...il [Survenant] porte alors sur l'existence routinière de ces derniers, sur leur médiocre sédentarisme et leur esprit casanier un jugement de valeur qui n'a plus rien de tendre ni d'indulgent.' (226).

Nonetheless thèy do not forget him after he has left, as more than one critic has shown. (Duquette, (5). 'Même absent, cet être étrange dérange aussi profondément l'ordre des choses et des hommes.' Leclerc, (40). 'Au Chenal du Moine, cependant, où sa présence ne laissait personne indifférent, il reste des traces de son passage, dans l'affection des uns et la haine des autres.') His effect on their community lingers on in the drinking of Joinville Provençal and in the secret hope of Angélina that one day the Survenant will return. He is still talked about, and his feats are remembered, but, in many ways, his influence has been profoundly disturbing and has seriously disrupted the Beauchemin family. Didace has been encouraged to marry a woman who is older than he thought and cannot give him the children that he longs for. His hopes that she and Alphonsine could work harmoniously together are shattered by the grasping nature of the Acayenne and the terror that Alphonsine has of being dispossessed. As she watches the Acayenne take over everything, even her baby who unhestitatingly prefers the warmth and comfort of the Acayenne's bosom to the bony discomfort of Alphonsine's, she becomes obsessed with her hatred of the incomer. The death of Amable is partly due to the influence of the Survenant whose example he tries to follow and, even more, to the arrival of the Acayenne, the replacement for the Survenant who introduces nothing but disharmony into the house. Didace loses some of his family pride with the gradual disappearance of his race. When he abandons the harvest to go with the strangers who want to go duck-shooting, it is a clear sign that he is less concerned with the future. The heart-attack which kills him is the direct result, and the death of the Acayenne soon after drives Alphonsine to madness. She cannot live with her guilty conscience and the knowledge that she did not do what she could to keep the Acayenne alive. Mary Jean Green is in no doubt that the Acayenne is wholly responsible for the collapse of Alphonsine (254).

> The direct agent of Phonsine's downfall is certainly the Acadian, who has brought about Amable's departure, alienated her daughter's affections, and threatened to cheat her out of her heritage.

This series of disasters leaves the six-year old Marie-Didace an orphan to be reared by Angélina, who can achieve motherhood only at second hand, while Marie-Didace's inheritance will be guarded for her by the parish under the leadership of Pierre-Côme, her godfather. Local solidarity comes to the fore to protect the land, but the name Beauchemin is doomed to disappear at either the marriage or the death of Marie-Didace.

The intrusion of a stranger as flamboyant and as alien as the Survenant into a small, settled community has a profound and disturbing effect on the lives of those with whom he comes into contact. As Lepage comments, nothing will ever be the same again (143).

> Après son passage, plus rien ne sera pareil pour ces sédentaires à qui il aura montré la voie de la modernité.

He reinvigorates those who are drawn to him, but he also arouses hostile and negative reactions in those who see him as a threat. The community is divided, and some are not sorry to see him depart. His lasting effect, however, is to introduce the Acayenne, a survenante, into the parish, and her influence is wholly negative as is suggested by Girouard who sees her as the incarnation of Thanatos (44) and by Baillie who argues that (116) 'Venant ne se contente pas de ravager le cœur d'Angélina Desmarais, c'est comme s'il intriguait pour que le père Didace fasse lui-même son malheur et celui des autres autour de lui. Une fois le dommage assuré, pour sûr il s'en ira...'. Her appearance promises warmth, comfort and happiness, but instead she is gradually shown to be deceitful, divisive and acquisitive. With the best of intentions the Survenant had paved the way for a wholly destructive force to enter the community, which makes it difficult to accept the interpretation of Françoise Maccabée-Iqbal, that the Survenant is a redeemer who leaves once his mission of redemption has been accomplished (248-56). The Survenant and his successor, the Survenante, bring the outside world into the closed community of Chenal du Moine, but Roy, perhaps, overemphasises the effect of the Survenant, as the people of Chenal du Moine remain very resistant to outside influences, particularly in *Le Survenant* (39).

> Grâce au Survenant, le Chenal du Moine n'est pas un monde clos. Il reste ouvert sur le monde extérieur et d'une certaine façon, son sort est lié à celui du monde extérieur.

Nevertheless, the Survenant and the Acayenne expose the weaknesses and the limitations of the parish and leave it shaken to its foundations. As Lepage has argued, a free spirit enters a world, which is frozen in its past, and offers its inhabitants the chance to escape (1992, 161).

Germaine Guèvremont introduit dans l'univers sclérosé du Chenal du Moine un homme totalement libre, dont le rôle fondamental consiste à inciter les personnages aliénés à secouer le joug de leur oppression.

This is indeed how Guèvremont herself envisaged her book - the traditional French parish disturbed by the entry of an outsider who brings with him a destructive modernity (Lepage, 1992, 152-3).

C'est la vieille paroisse qui garde à une province sa figure française...Mais qu'adviendrait-il si un élément étranger, humain et d'autant plus dangereux qu'il aurait autant de qualités que de défauts, soulevait dans la vieille paroisse, la poussière d'un mauvais modernisme?

Poussière sur la ville; André Langevin

André Langevin's second novel, *Poussière sur la ville*, published eight years after *Le Survenant* in 1953, marks a complete break with the *roman du terroir* or, if Guèvremont's own term is used, the *roman de la paroisse*. His novel is concerned with a survenant and a survenante, a young Montreal doctor, Alain Dubois and his new bride, Madeleine, who move to the small mining town of Macklin to set up his practice. The season is winter, and Macklin is dominated by the snow and the dust from the asbestos mines where the miners earn their living. It is a cold, ugly, dirty town whose inhabitants are intensely suspicious of incomers and seem to lead lives which reflect the joylessness and harshness of their surroundings as Jean-Claude Tardif demonstrates (246).

> Elle [Macklin] impose aux habitants une façon de vivre, silencieuse, implacable. Elle les oblige à se serrer les coudes, à faire cercle ensemble et à contrôler les ambitions de chacun. On isole au centre les indésirables avant de les rejeter.

Alain is the protégé of the ageing Doctor Lafleur who hopes that Alain will take over his practice, the best one in Macklin. From the start Madeleine, who is working-class, adapts to the town and the people better than Alain, whose background is solidly bourgeois. She is accepted more easily by the townspeople, particularly after she takes as her lover the handsomest young man in the town. Alain fails utterly to integrate, even when, as Gabrielle Pascal points out, he is offered the chance by three different people (6-7).

> Il [Alain Dublois] se voit offrir, à son arrivée à Macklin, trois intégrations différentes et se montre incapable de profiter d'aucune d'elles. Kouri, son voisin restaurateur, qu'il surnomme le Syrien, lui offre une amitié sincère à laquelle il ne sait pas répondre. Arthur Prévost, l'homme le plus important de la ville, lui propose une alliance avec les nantis de l'endroit, mais il le méprise, ne voyant en lui qu'un patron tyrannique qui se promène dans son magasin 'comme un planteur dans ses champs de coton'. Enfin, le docteur Lafleur envoie Alain chez ses malades pour lui permettre de se faire progressivement une clientèle personnelle. Mais, bouleversé par 'les figures sinistres' qui l'accueillent, celui-ci est incapable de sortir de lui-même et nourrit, par son silence, la méfiance paysanne de ses patients.

The tragic events of Alain's stay in Macklin are narrated in the first person so that the only point of view presented to the reader is that of Alain himself. All the other characters are seen through Alain's eyes, and their voices are mediated through him. As Réjean and Robidoux point out, the novelist is careful to keep at a distance: 'Le romancier ne nous impose pas sa présence dans *Poussière sur la ville.*' (128). It should be noted that André Brochu has a different point of view which stresses that the effect of the first person narrative is to allow the narrator to become the focus of attention (58).

> ...Alain n'est pas le véritable narrateur. Il est le titulaire purement formel de la narration, donc un narrateur artificiel, mais non toutefois gratuit ou arbitraire, car la narration à la première personne permet une focalisation maximale sur le personnage. Elle en fait le sujet absolu du *point de vue* narratif. Alain est ce regard posé sur tous et sur lui-même.

The reader has to trust the good faith and the accuracy of Alain's account, which is by no means unbiased, as Alain is concerned to prove to himself, his principal audience, the generosity and compassion which he showed to Madeleine. Alain is wracked by insecurity and self-doubt. He is, as critics have pointed out, an existentialist hero who, unlike Doctor Lafleur, lacks any religious faith and is nauseated by the cruelty and the pointlessness of man's existence. André Gaulin emphasises the dreariness of his outlook (158).

> Le héros existentialiste, Alain Dubois, devant la nausée où s'englue sa vie traduit bien son vague-à-l'âme fade comme de la poussière.

This view is modified by Alexandre Amprimoz who, while accepting the links between Langevin, on the one hand, and Sartre and Camus, on the other, shows how Langevin differentiates himself from his French predecessors. Langevin is writing after the war, and his hero is in love and married, whereas Roquentin and Meursault were bachelors indifferent to love (97-98). As Alain's time in Macklin is marked by both personal and professional disappointment culminating in the suicide of Madeleine and his own withdrawal from the town for three months, his perspective is understandably gloomy. The town and all the other characters are, therefore, seen through this haze of disappointment and depression, symbolised by the ever-present asbestos dust which covers the town, shut in by its circle of hills.

Falardeau points out that from the moment of their arrival in Macklin, which Langevin personifies so that the collectivity becomes another character in the book, Alain is aware that the town is watching him and Madeleine (126).

> Elle [Macklin] est plus que témoin de la tragédie qui s'insinue entre le docteur Alain Dubois et son épouse Madeleine. Elle s'y associe, la pénètre, l'accentue, l'oriente. Ce drame est vite devenu son drame.

As David Bond comments: 'There is a clear echo of Sartrean philosophy in this novel, and especially of the existentialist idea that all have an existence "in the eyes of others"' (21). The opening sentence brings this home to the reader.

> Une grosse femme, l'oeil mi-clos dans la neige, me dévisage froidement. Je la regarde moi aussi, sans la voir vraiment, comme si mon regard la transperçait et portait plus loin, très loin derrière elle. (p.11)

The difference in the quality of their gaze is revealing. Alain looks beyond the apparent object of his gaze which he does not really see. He is detached from his surroundings, lost in his own world of misery and suspicion. As Paul Socken shows, Alain has trouble both literally and metaphorically in seeing other people even when, as with *la grosse femme*, he is apparently looking at them. His inability to see prepares the reader for his difficulty in communicating with those around him, even those like Kouri, who tries to communicate with him (177).

> Alain's alienation, to which we have alluded earlier, finds dramatic expression in this first page as Kouri's attempt at communication is perceived with difficulty both by the reader and by Alain. The reader thereby gains insight into the philosophical dilemma at the heart of the novel - the distance between Alain and the world around him.

The woman, representing Macklin, is observing him closely, looking for proof of her suspicion that he is either drunk or mad. Wherever he goes, he is made aware of this watchfulness on the part of the other characters. He has to run the gauntlet of the appraising stares of the miners in Kouri's restaurant when he goes there to buy cigarettes and to see if Madeleine is there on her own, behaviour which is not acceptable in Macklin for a doctor's wife. When Alain tries to escape from the unhappiness of his life by going to drown his sorrows in the local hotel, Arthur Prévost has no hesitation in warning Alain that people of their class in Macklin do not behave like that. Not only has he been seen getting drunk in the hotel, the word has been carried back to the people of influence. His attempt to escape from his troubles has been futile. As Bednarski argues, the visit to the hotel has resulted in a disaster (221).

> Il y [l'hôtel] tente de s'évader en se saoûlant le dimanche de la découverte de la trahison de Madeleine. Cette visite provoque le scandale.

Alain knows perfectly well that he has flouted convention, but he has no patience with the requirements of small-town society. He ignored the discreet hints of the hotel manager and reacted badly to Kouri's attempt to save him from himself. Prévost's warnings are well-meant but are received with hostility. As Prévost has lent Alain money and sees him as a potentially profitable investment, Alain has no hesitation in attributing purely mercenary motives to the warning. He does not seem to consider that the older man might also be interested in his well-being. Later in the book there is a second interview between the two men when Madeleine's adultery is causing a scandal in the town. Alain is openly hostile despite the weakness of his position. At the end of the interview Prévost states his position bluntly.

> - J'ai les moyens de vous briser! Je m'intéresse à vous, je vous aide, je vous mets en garde et vous le prenez sur ce ton. Nous nous reverrons, docteur. Et vous aurez peut-être la tête un peu moins haute. (172)

His patience and good-will have been exhausted. He does not understand the attitude of Alain and, having tried to befriend him, he is now all the more hostile and ready to use his financial might to bring Alain to heel or to break him. Alain attempts to plan some form of resistance, but in fact all that he can hope for is that something will turn up. 'En quelques mois il peut arriver tellement de choses' (173). The estrangement and lack of understanding between the two men are clearly visible, but Alain has also failed to understand how Macklin works. When he tries to raise more money at the bank, he fails. He had not anticipated that the bank would prefer to ally itself with Prévost, who is a far better financial risk than a struggling, young doctor, as Falardeau points out (141).

The arrival of the young doctor and his beautiful, red-haired wife in Macklin is deeply unsettling for both the town and the couple. Alain admits that he and Madeleine did not know each other well before their marriage. Madeleine had been pushed towards the marriage by her mother, the widow of 'un employé de tramway' (18) who was dazzled by the idea of her daughter marrying a doctor. He himself had been captivated by Madeleine's beauty, in particular by her flame-coloured hair, which makes her stand out wherever she goes and by which, in Pascal's eyes, she is defined (70). 'Le personnage de Madeleine est entièrement défini par cette flamme rousse à laquelle Alain s'est brûlé.' Pascal also comments on the importance of the colour of Madeleine's hair, the symbol simultaneously of her fatal beauty and her desire to be free, a colour of which Langevin is very fond, to judge by its appearance in his other novels (69-70). Perhaps, as Pascal suggests, Alain was attracted not only by her beauty but also by the fact that she was from a lower class and a friend of his disgraced cousin (45).

> Elle était...l'amie d'une cousine dont on s'entretenait à voix basse dans la famille Dubois. Et c'est cette désapprobation familiale dont elle souffrait qui semble avoir attiré Alain Dubois.

Once in Macklin Alain quickly discovers that Madeleine's untameable nature, her refusal to be confined by convention make her quite unsuited to the dull routine of life as the wife of a small-town doctor. Alain realises that he is unable to satisfy her need for entertainment and excitement, and, as Tardif suggests, that he is losing her (243).

> Il cherche ardemment à comprendre Madeleine. Incapable de partager, incapable de communiquer, trop éloigné d'elle, il sent qu'elle lui échappe...

He cannot reawaken the sexual pleasure that they had together when he seduced her before their marriage. Significantly he recalls this scene of happiness, sunlight and warmth in a flashback which contrasts with the distress, the snow and the cold by which they are surrounded in Macklin. Madeleine seems indifferent to the watchful eyes of Macklin. She does not feel threatened in this environment, where she can hold her own with the miners and other workers.

> Ils [les mineurs] sont ici [chez Kouri] chez eux et la présence de Madeleine ne leur paraît pas insolite. Depuis trois mois, ils se sont habitués à elle, l'ont reconnue peut-être comme de la même race qu'eux. (63)

Alain, from the first encounter in Kouri's restaurant where his authority as a husband is challenged, realises that he is failing to conform to the behaviour expected of a man.

> En ne faisant rien moi-même pour la défendre, je leur [aux mineurs] cédais le terrain sur le seul plan qui les intéressait vraiment, celui de la virilité. (33)

Arthur Prévost expresses concisely the bewilderment of the townspeople as they watch the young doctor accept his public cuckolding by his wife and even permit her to entertain her lover in the house while he is there.

> - Votre propre conduite...heuh...est assez étrange. Nous ne comprenons pas votre attitude qui prête à ...à discussion.
> - Que voulez-vous dire?
> J'avais la voix sifflante, cette fois, il s'en est rendu compte. Il a abandonné une délicatesse qui le gênait aux entournures.
> - Mais quand on est un homme on ne tolère pas l'amant de sa femme chez soi. Tout le monde vous lâche à ce point-là. Mais vous n'avez aucun orgueil! (172)

The scandal caused by the doctor's wife taking a lover is almost eclipsed by the scandal of the doctor accepting the affair.

Throughout the book Alain is sensitive about his masculinity. He knows that physically he seems a poor specimen beside the miners, although he seeks frequent reassurance in the mirror that his physique is acceptable.

> Je me déshabille en me regardant vaguement dans la glace. Pas pour me rassurer. C'est machinal chez moi, tous les soirs...Un gars de la ville, bien sûr. A côté des mineurs, je dois paraître malingre. Mais c'est robuste. Je me surprends à faire jouer les muscles. (24)

The mere fact that he has to deny that he is seeking reassurance alerts the reader to his lack of confidence which, according to Réjean and Robidoux, stems mainly from the infidelity of Madeleine (135-36).

> Toute l'inquiétude d'Alain, sa confusion devant les événements, son incapacité d'agir, la tension qui monte en lui à mesure qu'avance l'aventure romanesque, proviennent de l'infidélité de Madeleine, du mutisme de la jeune femme, qui ne se confie jamais à son mari et qui ne lui laisse, pour comprendre, que l'évidence du geste accompli.

This does not take into account the fact that Alain is already seeking reassurance before he is aware that Madeleine is unfaithful. Her infidelity makes much worse a lack of confidence which was already present, and his narcissism betrays the inner weakness that he is trying to conceal from himself. Aware that he cannot satisfy Madeleine sexually, that he cannot give her the excitement that she craves, that he cannot compete with the miners physically and that no one, not even Doctor Lafleur can understand his behaviour, Alain seeks refuge in two ways. He discovers that alcohol is an effective method of dulling the pain that he feels at his wife's infidelity and he rapidly becomes an alcoholic, although as Pascal points out, the relief is both temporary and an illusion (78). '…l'alcool vise à effacer une situation de conflit, mais le secours qu'il apporte est illusoire.' When he has to try to deliver a hydrocephalic baby while drunk, the family immediately notices the stink of whisky. As he has to kill the baby, a boy, to save the mother, his reputation is thereafter in tatters throughout the community, which does not accept his attempt at self-justification. He also seeks refuge in pity, not so much for himself, although self-pity is certainly present, as he is beginning to recognise by the end of the book: 'Je m'apitoyais sur moi-même' (208), but in pity for Madeleine. He takes considerable pride in this approach which marks him out from the cruel, hard people of Macklin. They, for their part, see it as further proof of his weakness. Macklin has no room for compassion, and those who cannot defend themselves are despised, as Tardif shows (247). 'Dans cette ville il n'y a pas de place pour la pitié et encore moins pour les faibles.' At first Alain feels pity only for Madeleine who is so desperately unhappy, but after her death he returns to Macklin determined to conquer the town by pity.

> Je resterai, contre toute la ville. Je les forcerai à m'aimer. La pitié qui m'a si mal réussi avec Madeleine, je les en inonderai. J'ai un beau métier où la pitié peut sourdre sans cesse sans qu'on l'appelle. Je continue mon combat. (213)

Critics are divided on how to interpret this ending. Throughout the book Alain has shown himself to be unable to judge others accurately. He has repeatedly tried to avoid understanding what was happening around him. He was very slow to realise that Madeleine was unfaithful. He was surprised by the reactions of the townspeople to his behaviour. As Réjean and Roubidoux point out, for all that Alain is an acute observer, he constantly turns back to his own reactions and thoughts (135).

> Le personnage-narrateur notera avec une minutie scrupuleuse tous les faits qui s'étalent sous ses yeux, interprétera chacun des gestes, retiendra chacune des paroles de Madeleine et, surtout, il se repliera constamment sur lui-même afin d'étudier ses propres réactions pour choisir l'attitude à prendre.

He knows, as he and Doctor Lafleur have said on more than one occasion, that the people of Macklin are hard on themselves and hard on others. The first patients, who come to his surgery when he reopens it after his three month absence following the death of Madeleine, have come to condemn her. Alain could be indulging in self-deception or, as Betty Bednarski suggests, it is only through pity that he has the strength to continue to live (238). 'Dans l'univers d'Alain Dubois, il reste pourtant un petit espoir – celui qu'offre la pitié.' Gabrielle Pascal, however, sees his decision to remain quite differently. In her eyes his behaviour is typical of Langevin's heroes who deliberately choose to torture themselves (39).

> ...Alain Dubois choisit de rester à Macklin, la ville dont les habitants l'ont rejeté...Chez Langevin, les personnages ne souhaitent finalement rien d'autre que de nourrir leur blessure originelle. Leur masochisme est incurable.

David Bond sees it rather as a limited optimism which enables the characters to face the absurdity of life with courage. The signs of pity that Kouri and Jim show at the end of the book are encouraging. Bond describes them as the most unlikely characters to feel pity (26).

> Alain's refusal to despair, while knowing that he cannot win any lasting victory, shows a limited optimism, a belief that it is possible to face the absurd with courage. Perhaps the most hopeful aspect of the work is its suggestion that pity can be felt by the most unlikely people [Kouri and Jim].

In fact, they are, after Doctor Lafleur, the ones most likely to sympathise with Alain. Kouri has shown, throughout the book, signs of being prepared to intervene on Alain's side, even although he usually kept himself to himself. Jim had provided Alain with some support when they went to the scene of Madeleine's suicide. Alain is undoubtedly full of courage and even hope as he prepares to resume his career in Macklin, resisting both the suggestion offered by Doctor

Lafleur to move to another town and the offer of Kouri to fund such a move. Doctor Lafleur warns him that Macklin will never forgive him.

> -...Il y a plus de quarante ans que je les connais. Ils sont sans pitié, pour eux-mêmes et pour les autres. On vous tient pour le seul coupable. Vous seul êtes indemne...
> -Indemne!
> Le cri m'avait échappé. J'eus peine à ne pas pleurer de stupéfaction.
> - Pour eux, vous n'avez rien souffert. Vous leur semblez être de connivence avec votre malheur. (208)

The town has already passed judgement and it seems unlikely, to say the least, that Alain's feelings of pity will alter their conclusion. As Gaulin points out, their feelings are completely different (160).

> Les Macklinois, eux, ne comprennent rien à la pitié. Ils sont durs, courageux, cruels pour les faibles...Ils accusent le docteur Dubois de lâcheté...

Hope is there, but it is illusory, another example of Alain's self-deception. He is doomed to repeat the vicious circle of his existence, trying and failing to win over the people of Macklin, as Pascal argues when she rejects the interpretation of Gilles Marcotte that Alain shows 'une généreuse pitié'. She describes his mood as 'une complaisance masochiste', seeing his struggle as futile and, indeed, self-indulgent. '...Alain Dubois entreprend une lutte perdue d'avance, un exploit impossible. Il poursuit un rêve qui le valorise' (49). It is hard to see why Alain should have any grounds for optimism, and the critics who see Alain as a naïve, deluded dreamer, enjoying his misery and feeling of rejection are the more convincing.

Madeleine was even more affected by the move to Macklin than Alain. She had married a man whom she did not really know to move from Montreal to a small town where she knew no one. As Alain realised, the prospect of the move and the change excited her but the reality quickly turned sour. The town was ugly, the flat over his consulting room was unattractive, and Madeleine quickly realised that Alain was facing stiff competition in Macklin. During a short walk she counted four other doctors' plates. No housewife, she did not find the challenge of making an attractive home out of the flat interesting. Without the help of their maid, Thérèse, the Dubois would live in squalor. There was nothing to do in Macklin apart from going to the cinema or passing the time by drinking sodas and listening to the jukebox in Kouri's restaurant, an activity which exposed her to the curious scrutiny of its mainly male clientele.

> Dans le restaurant, tous les hommes n'avaient d'yeux que pour elle. Les visages fermés, rudes considéraient calmement ma femme qui, entre deux bouchées, soutenait ces regards avec une tranquille assurance. (32)

The ladies of Macklin, and, by her marriage to one of the doctors Madeleine has become one of them, do not go to Kouri's, but Madeleine enjoys breaking the rules, because, as Amprimoz comments, it is her way of hitting back: 'Madeleine a un caractère agressif et elle répond aux diverses provocations' (161). Through the jukebox and even more the films Madeleine is seeking to escape the drabness of Macklin and of her life. Too romantic and excitable to be satisfied with the dull mediocrity which seems to be her future, she lives a fantasy life through the films and the sentimental pop music which Alain cannot share and does not understand. Christine Tellier offers a very convincing explanation of this failure on the part of the young doctor to empathise with his wife (577).

> Le médecin ne comprend pas son épouse, qui symbolise un monde de désirs et d'émotions, alors qu'il se définit lui-même comme un homme de raison.

Madeleine's escape from reality is, however, illusory, as Bond points out, for all the means which she uses fail her, so that any happiness which she thinks she achieves is unreal and of short duration (24). Despite her rejection of reality she fits into the town quite easily in a way that Alain with his self-doubt and his conventional outlook never can. According to Tellier, she is as pitiless as the people of Macklin (578). It is no surprise that a young and beautiful newcomer who behaves so outrageously should attract the attention of the local Don Juan, Richard Hétu, who is everything that Alain is not - good-looking, muscular, successful with women and from the same class as Madeleine. The town is at first sympathetic to the lovers, as Ducrocq-Poirier states (609).

> Madeleine échappe complètement à son mari et se laissera séduire par un homme de son niveau, le camionneur Richard Hêtu avec la complicité tacite de toute la ville.

In her affair with Richard, Madeleine seems to be playing a role in one of the films of which she is so fond. She sees herself as a tragic figure loving a man who does not love her. She knows that he took her only because she offered herself to him. At the same time she is very aware that Alain loves her, and she tells him that she has no wish to hurt him.

Richard's rejection of her comes as a shattering blow to her, driving her to flight. Alain watches uncomprehending as she prepares her departure for Montreal. He is not even suspicious when she refuses to let him drive her to the station on the specious grounds that there might be patients coming to the surgery. The shock for him is immense when he understands the depth of her deception. Under his eyes she had planned her exit so that it would resemble one of her films. Having stolen Kouri's revolver, she plans to shoot Richard and then turn the gun on herself for a tragic finale, but her plan miscarries. Richard is only wounded and she is left to die alone in the snow outside his house where the door is firmly shut against her. The neighbours form a circle round her through which Alain has to break to reach her, and only he and Jim, the taxi-driver, show any emotion over the corpse. The Macklinois are detached spectators.

Madeleine's short stay in Macklin changes her from a confident, beautiful young woman, capable of turning all heads to a tearful, distressed, adulterous wife torn between love and guilt. She can see no future with Alain, and she has lost her self-respect with the realisation that she has given herself to Richard for nothing. She is indifferent to the dissension that she has caused in the town. In her own way she is hard like the Macklinois, but she has tried to escape from the harsh life of Macklin by living the life of her favourite film stars. She has failed to make her dream become reality, and at the end there is nothing left for her but death.

The intervention of Madeleine in his life changes everything for Richard. His previous affairs with girls from Macklin seem to have left him cheerful and untroubled, to judge by his first encounter with Alain Dubois. He reacts immediately, however, to the name and barely acknowledges Alain's existence. Richard is extremely uncomfortable during his affair with Madeleine despite the fact that Alain can offer him no competition, as Marie-Lyne Piccione points out (1980, 69).

> Beau comme un acteur de cinéma, véritable colosse, Richard Hétre [sic], l'amant de Madeleine, ne laisse aucune chance au mari qui avoue lui-même paraître malingre.

He cannot adjust to Alain's unconventional behaviour and is out of his depth when faced with an intellectual. He is never allowed to speak in his own voice by the narrator. Indeed, as Tellier points out, neither of the lovers can speak to the audience directly, as everything is reported by Alain (579).

> Madeleine n'a pas de voix propre dans le roman; ni son amant, Richard Hétu, un homme du peuple comme elle, qui n'a pour sa part aucune réplique.

Like everyone else in Macklin he does not understand Alain's policy of tolerance and pity, a policy which Pascal explains as an unconscious attempt by Alain to annexe Richard's physical strength (57).

> S'il [Alain Dubois] tolère son rival chez lui, c'est peut-être parce qu'il espère inconsciemment, par un effet de sorcellerie intime, s'emparer de cette force d'exister qui lui manque...'

Richard is ill at ease in Madeleine's sitting room with the pink sofa which is too feminine and too small for him.

> Lui, gauche, trop grand et trop fruste pour ce divan rose, timide et ne sachant trop ce qui lui arrive. Lorsque j'entre il regarde toujours à ses pieds, le visage pourpre. (169)

Alain suspects that Richard has a guilty conscience which contrasts with the carefree lorry driver whose lorry was blocking the road to the hospital a few weeks earlier, when Alain did not know who he was. This would help to explain why he abandons Madeleine so readily when the curé moves to break up the affair. Apparently without hesitation, Richard accepts the proposed fiancée, a niece of Arthur Prévost, and a former girl friend. The town is satisfied.

> Le curé a fiancé hier Richard Hétu à une jeune fille qu'il a dénichée je ne sais où. Un homme énergique, le curé...Il semble que Richard ait longtemps vu cette jeune fille avant de connaître Madeleine. Mieux encore, elle est nièce d'Arthur Prévost. Un beau mariage pour le printemps. Richard est beau. On trouvera encore que sa fiancé a de la chance. (180)

For Richard there are further trials in store; Madeleine's attempt to murder him, followed by the inquest where he says as little as possible. By the spring after Madeleine's death Richard's life will have changed greatly. He will have survived a turbulent affair which made him the talk of the town, an attempt on his life and a hurried engagement to a member of one of the leading families in Macklin. By the summer Richard will be respectably married into Macklin society.

The other male characters are also affected by the troubles of Alain and Madeleine. Kouri, the Syrian restaurateur, finds himself involved in spite of himself. Hitherto, the Syrian has managed to keep himself detached from the town, withdrawing as much as possible to his house on the lake at the other end of the valley. Almost against his better judgement he is drawn into Alain's affairs. He indicates to Alain that Madeleine is in the restaurant by herself. When he sees Alain in the hotel, getting steadily more and more drunk, he intervenes and escorts his car back to Macklin. At the end when Alain returns to Macklin, Kouri quite unexpectedly both offers to fund Alain if he should set up his practice elsewhere and invites Alain to come and spend some time at the house by the lake. After receiving this invitation Alain describes Kouri as 'mon ange gardien' (210) which leads Pascal to suggest that Alain is seeking his lost father (who died when Alain was five) in Kouri (13). Clearly Alain sees Kouri as a source of support, but Kouri does not intend to take on the role of a replacement father-figure, although such involvement in the life of others on his part is unprecedented. The Dubois have changed the life and the role of Kouri as much as those of Richard.

Arthur Prévost is not so greatly affected. He has the discomfort of seeing one of his money-making schemes going sadly awry, as Doctor Dubois turns out to be a very poor investment for his money. The tragic circumstances of the death of Madeleine also make it more difficult for him to exert the pressure that he would like to use on Alain, although before her death the latter was just beginning to discover the full extent of the power of Prévost in Macklin. Prévost has nonetheless had the disagreeable experience of seeing his well-meant advice rejected and a man whom he was trying to help turn against him. As the uncle of Richard's fiancée, he has, presumably, been involved in the Curé's outwitting of Madeleine. His troubles may be minor compared with those of Alain and Madeleine but he has been changed too. As Alain still owes him a lot of money, he cannot shake off the unpleasant events of the previous year and detach himself from the young doctor who has turned out to be such a disappointment. For the moment, at least, Arthur Prévost is tied to the Dubois and the scandal associated with them.

The Curé has had to face a severe challenge to his authority in the town. Madeleine and Alain have created a flagrant scandal, the effect of which on his parishioners is feared by the curé. When he challenges Alain over his policy of tolerance which nobody, least of all the Curé, understands, he is troubled by Alain's questions about the bases of his judgement, which he is not used to having challenged, particularly by a non-believer (who is, as Bond shows, typical of Langevin's heroes (23). 'Alain is another of Langevin's seekers after the absolute who rejects the injustice of God...'). The lack of understanding between the priest and the young doctor is total. According to Amprimoz, Langevin signals this by the failure of Alain to understand the meaning of the Curé's gestures as he tries to flag Alain down as he drives through the town (99).

> Il est clair que l'homme et le prêtre qui ne se comprennent pas au niveau des gestes (des signes, c'est-à-dire des symboles immédiats) ne se comprendront guère mieux au niveau verbal.

It is yet another example of Alain's distance from his surroundings and the people of the town. As the Curé is a man from Macklin, he can neither understand nor forgive Alain's behaviour.

> Il n'a pas pitié et ne comprend pas la pitié parce qu'il est de leur race à eux, dur, courageux et cruel pour les faibles. (165)

As a priest, he is determined to protect his flock from the example of sinfulness which Madeleine is setting. He acts with a speed and an efficacity which destroy the Dubois who find themselves almost isolated and powerless in a town which has closed ranks against them. The Curé triumphantly meets the challenge to his authority, but ultimately at the cost of Madeleine's life.

Alain's patron, Doctor Lafleur, does not escape either. He has picked Alain as his replacement. He is getting old and is less and less able to cope with the appalling climate of Macklin. Like Prévost, he sees the need for an able young doctor in the community but he had not reckoned with Alain's inability to integrate with the people of Macklin or Madeleine's boredom. Instead of being able to hand over his practice gradually to Alain, Doctor Lafleur finds himself forced to support him emotionally and to some extent financially, as he watches Alain's career disintegrate. Like Kouri he is careful never to judge but for him there is the disappointment of seeing his chosen successor ruin his chances. Also like Kouri, he is a possible and rather more probable father-figure for Alain, as Bond suggests (23). 'Alain has no father himself and obviously sees Lafleur in this role.' Bond also suggests that Langevin's own life can be linked to that of his heroes, as Langevin had to spend some of his early years in an orphanage (7). At the end of the book Doctor Lafleur advises Alain to go elsewhere as the people of Macklin will never forgive him. It is advice which Alain rejects, outraged that he has been judged without a hearing. Doctor Lafleur repeats that he will never be forgiven and the town will never understand the only terms which he could use to defend himself. In their eyes he is *lâche*, and life is not long enough to disabuse them of that idea. Their conversation is interrupted by Kouri, and Doctor Lafleur leaves, continuing his policy of handing over his patients to him in the hope that Alain can establish his own practice. He has greatly aged during Alain's absence, as even the self-absorbed Alain notices. The events of the winter have taken their toll on him physically.

Even the taxi-driver, Jim, is affected by the death of Madeleine. All winter Jim maintains his attitude of detached cynicism, making a little trouble when he feels like it. He and Madeleine do not have any affection for each other, nor does he seem greatly concerned to act in Alain's interests. Nonetheless, when Madeleine is lying dead in the snow outside the Hétu house, it is Jim who brings the green blanket to cover her. The bystanders will not move, and the Hétu are all shut up in their house with the wounded Richard. The sign that Jim has really been affected comes right at the end when Alain suddenly sees him drunk for the first time.

> Je n'en crois pas mes yeux. Le gros Jim rentre dans sa cabane en titubant. Est-ce qu'il s'humanise? Il se saoûle maintenant. (p. 213)

Like Kouri, Jim has been drawn into the affairs of the Dubois which have left their mark on him. He has not been able to maintain his cynical detachment.

The people who seem to be least affected are the townspeople in general. In one way the townspeople are represented by Thérèse, the efficient and discreet maid of the Dubois, who is in her own way as much a spectator as Alain. She is in the flat with the young couple and seems to be in the confidence of Madeleine. Like the rest of the Macklinois, Thérèse remains a mysterious figure to Alain although he appreciates her attentiveness and her good nature. He admits that without her presence, the Dubois household would not survive even in appearance. As Réjean and Robidoux note, she and Jim watch continuously as Alain and Madeleine tear themselves apart (132).

> Deux personnages en particulier semblent délégués, dans la forme du roman, à incarner la présence active et troublante de la ville dans le drame d'Alain et de Madeleine: Jim, le chauffeur de taxi, «le scrutateur des consciences du pays», et Thérèse, l'énigmatique servante.

At the end of the book she fades back into the mass of Macklinois, as inscrutable as ever. Alain has even less interest in her than in Jim whose unexpected drunkenness catches his attention and, consequently, her personality never emerges from behind her smiling, good-humoured mask. She differs from the rest of the people only in that she does not seem ill-diposed to Alain and is the only friend of Madeleine in Macklin as well as being her maid.

While Thérèse, who knows Alain and Madeleine better than the rest of the townspeople, may feel some sympathy for them, the townspeople en masse are unmoved. Alain and Docteur Lafleur always refer to them as a unit, so that the reader is constantly aware of their massed ranks in the background. Alain is aware of their hostility, their watchfulness and their readiness to close ranks against the strangers. Madeleine temporarily gains acceptance as someone who belongs to the same class but Alain never does. At the end the position has worsened. According to Doctor Lafleur the townspeople will neither forget nor forgive. They have hardened their hearts against him. His decision to stay is, in part, a new beginning to win them over by his pity for them where he had so signally failed to win them over before. He does not take into account the fact that although he is prepared to start again, the evidence suggests that the Macklinois are not. The name Dubois now has a past attached to it which Alain cannot easily throw off. Doctor Lafleur has known the people of Macklin for forty years and is convinced that Alain will never be accepted.

The Dubois are survenants just like Le Survenant and L'Acayenne (Madeleine even has the same red hair as Guèvremont's characters), but Langevin has added new facets to the theme of a stranger arriving in town. His characters find themselves embroiled in problems of class, sex and social identity to a much greater degree than those of

Guèvremont. It is also possible to see Alain Dubois as a symbol of the Québécois themselves who, in the 1950s, were under the double yoke of the Duplessis régime and the anglophone Canadians, so that, for Jean Filiatraut, Alain represents a defeated and dispirited people who are accepting their fate as victims of a more powerful and successful race (188). 'C'est un masochiste. Voilà peut-être pourquoi il est fait à notre image, à une certaine image de notre peuple, qui est un peuple asservi...'. The outcome is more violent and more tragic than in the novel of Guèvremont. Above all, the people who are most affected by the arrival of the survenant and the survenante in Macklin are the couple themselves. By the end of the novel Madeleine is dead, the victim of the tension between her fantasy life of film and pop music, on the one hand, and her real life of disappointment and drabness on the other. Alain has had his inner weaknesses exposed and has had to face his complete failure both professionally and personally. His decision to continue in Macklin can be seen as either courageous or masochistic, depending on the extent to which the reader accepts Alain's assessment of the situation. Many critics, like Jean Filiatraut, are in no doubt about the real situation (188-89).

> Notre héros est un faible; il pratique avec trop de passion ce que Georges Duhamel appelle quelque part le "spectorat"...le docteur s'y complaît par masochisme, il se regarde souffrir et se laisse détruire, c'est un impuissant.

Given the clear opinion of Doctor Lafleur and Alain's own powers of self-deception, it is more than probable that the attempt to win over the Macklinois is doomed to failure. Indeed, Ducrocq-Poirier sees no hope for him (610). 'Mis en demeure après le scandale de quitter Macklin, il emportera avec lui ses habitudes d'alcoolique.' Alain will not succeed in breaking the circle of fate which has surrounded him since his arrival in the town and which is symbolised by the mountains which enclose the town and cut it off from the rest of the province. Voisine sees the circle as closing in again on Alain's return to Macklin after the temporary break caused by his withdrawal from the town, although she does add that Alain will try break out of the circle by using the weapons of love and pity associated with his profession (210). 'Enfin, le cercle d'hostilité que la ville avait formé autour du couple, momentanément rompu par l'absence d'Alain après la mort de Madeleine, se referme de nouveau autour de lui, dès son retour.' As Pascal has said, the novel describes the death of a marriage too hastily concluded (43). Voisine comments that Alain himself seems to realise that the marriage was based entirely on his lust for Madeleine and her acceptance of his desire (208).

> Les époux ne réussissent pas à établir entre eux les liens qui leur permettraient d'accéder au bonheur dans et par l'amour. Alain nous apprend que les éléments d'union entre eux se situent essentiellement au plan physique.

For Alain the marriage was based mainly on Madeleine's beauty and the challenge posed by her elusiveness, while Madeleine was manoeuvred into the marriage by the social ambitions of her mother with ultimately fatal consequences, in that, as Pascal suggests, the social ambitions of the mother of Madeleine for her daughter drove her to revolt, a revolt which ends with her suicide (31). The reticence, soon to become hostility, of Macklin coupled with its dreary atmosphere and lack of entertainments quickly destroyed any chance of success in the marriage. Alain was too inhibited to take the sort of action which might have retained the interest of Madeleine and far too slow to realise how quickly Madeleine was drifting away from him.

The arrival of the survenant couple in Macklin brings out clearly the class divisions in post-war Canada. The bourgeois doctor is ill at ease amongst the workers of Macklin who are prepared to pay for his professional skill but have little respect for him as a man. He lacks the self-confidence to cope with their silent contempt and is at a loss when his wife openly defies him and eventually chooses a lover from the ranks of the men who have weighed him in the balance and found him wanting. Madeleine, on the other hand, is from the same background, as the miners, and even if they disapprove of her conduct, they have little trouble in accepting her. Alain realises that the town is mildly flattered that she should choose one of its sons as her lover in preference to her husband, the intruding bourgeois from Montréal.

> La ville entière penche pour Madeleine. Ma femme a préféré un de ses enfants et ma femme est de leur race...Moi le mari, je suis l'intrus. (138)

The town is shocked by the indiscretion of Madeleine who makes no effort to conceal her affair, but the men are even more shocked by what they see as the weakness of Alain when he fails to eject Richard from the house or, at least, take steps to see that Madeleine is brought to heel. His attempts to escape his problems through alcohol are also noticed and, because his failure to deliver the baby who is hydrocephalic is attributed to his drunkenness, this too becomes a cause for condemnation. The Dubois disturb the town through their failure to observe the norms of conventional behaviour partly because of the class divide and partly because of their sexual behaviour. Alain has to be held primarily responsible because the Macklinois do not understand him. They can understand the behaviour of Madeleine even if, in the end, they do not accept it. Alain's policy of tolerance and pity is totally alien to them, and what they do not understand, they despise.

On a philosophical level there is a great divide between Alain and the people of Macklin. Alain's behaviour and attitudes are outside the experience of the men of Macklin (no Macklin women, apart from Thérèse and some patients, appear), even of those, like Doctor Lafleur, who value Alain as a promising young doctor. The people of Macklin are hard on themselves and hard on others. They enjoy themselves with difficulty as Alain observes during the preparations for Christmas.

> La gigantesque mise en scène de Noël n'est plus qu'un décor troué et lacéré sur une scène abandonnée. Cela fait lendemain de fête, avec un peu d'amertume et la tristesse de sentir que les choses sont si peu éternelles. Pourtant, les promeneurs sont nombreux des deux côtés de la rue Green, les bras embarrassés de colis, les visages fatigués, nerveux. Pendant une nuit ils se tiendront éveillés à penser qu'il leur faut être heureux et le sommeil viendra avant le bonheur. (135)

He can only withstand the pressure of their hostility by refusing to resist, by becoming inert so that his opponents waste their strength uselessly. This tactic and his resort to the whisky bottle enable Alain to find the strength to stay in the town, convincing himself that his love for Madeleine is being expressed through his pity for her and his readiness to indulge her need for freedom, which had originally attracted him. He is, however, as Pascal notes, utterly alone like many other characters in Langevin's books (40). Macklin is still a town where the Curé is powerful. Doctor Lafleur is a practising Christian who is supported by his faith through the painful moments of his profession. Neither the Curé nor the doctor can understand Alain's rejection of their faith and, even if they are not able to counter all his arguments, their own faith remains unshaken, although Marcotte does not see the conflict as taking place in the novel (170).

> Quand le roman commence, les jeux sont faits, les personnages se meuvent dans un milieu intérieur où, semble-t-il, jamais l'interrogation de la foi n'a surgi. Dans *Poussière sur la ville* d'André Langevin par exemple, le personnage principal oppose son agnosticisme à la foi du vieux médecin et du curé, mais le combat, en lui-même, est terminé depuis longtemps.

They put their trust in God to whom they pray and neither of them believes that earthly happiness is the ultimate goal of life on earth. Alain rejects the God of cruelty, whom Marcotte describes as *le père cruel* (57).

> Son Dieu, le Dieu contre lequel il revendique, n'est que celui de la colère, la projection d'une absence cruellement ressentie. Il est resté pour lui...le *père cruel*; il l'est aussi pour les personnages chrétiens du roman. La foi du docteur Lafleur – qui ne manque pas de grandeur, du reste – est une foi aveugle, celle d'un homme en lutte contre la misère d'ici-bas et qui, vaincu, ne sait que prier dans le noir. Dieu de justice et de colère, également, celui du curé de Macklin: "*Je n'ai jamais cru et je ne croirai jamais au bonheur sur terre*". Pour qui, comme le jeune médecin, croit que "*la liberté c'est de pouvoir se rendre au bout de son bonheur*", toutes les avenues sont fermées qui conduisent à un tel dieu.

Gaulin suggests that Alain Dubois represents the agnostic point of view of Langevin himself (153), '...l'un des premiers agnostiques [Langevin] dans un pays qui possède une longue tradition chrétienne...Dans son univers romanesque, Dieu est mort.' Influenced by writers such as Sartre and Camus, Langevin has linked the theme of the survenant to the questions of death and human suffering, of revolt against the established conventions of society, as Bond states (5). In Macklin the victims of this revolt are the survenant and the survenante who find themselves far less powerful than the forces of the established order which are arrayed against them.

Gaulin argues that Alain is a sort of secular saint (159).

> Aussi Alain Dubois est-il celui qui représente le mieux l'humanisme langevinien; une pitié riche qui constitue une forme laïque de sainteté.

Brochu (60) ('...c'est la pitié, qui fait de Dubois une sorte de saint laïque, selon un formule cher à Camus') and Bond (25) ('Alain's pity is presented as a kind of humanism, and he himself as the closest thing to a saint in a world without God') are of the same opinion. According to Bond Alain's pity is a revolt against the absurdity of the pain and suffering of this world, and it is this revolt which turns the novel into a novel of hope (25-26). Pascal, on the other hand, believes that the heroes of Langevin are permanently on the margins of society (8). ('...le personnage de Langevin ne réussit jamais à sortir de la marginalité des exclus.') She also considers that they are condemned by their lack of a father figure to suffer an identity crisis which renders them unable to assert themselves, especially in their emotional relationships (59). Beaver, too, believes that Langevin's heroes are powerless to defeat their destiny, and in the context of Langevin's other novels this seems the most convincing interpretation (197). 'Malgré tous leurs efforts pour être les auteurs des drames dans lesquels ils jouent, ils doivent à la fin se soumettre au destin qu'on leur a choisi.'

In *Poussière sur la ville* Langevin has contrasted the traditional Quebec where religion and convention still ruled with the new, questioning attitude of the post-war period. At the time of writing when Duplessis was still solidly in power, the traditionalists were able to defeat the challenge posed by an interloper like Dubois who, in the eyes of many, represents the new generation of Québécois. Gaulin expresses this point of view (161). 'Alain Dubois est un authentique et douloureux Québécois d'après "la mort de Dieu".' The ending of the book shows that Alain still has hope that his pity will win over the people of Macklin, but the discussion with Doctor Lafleur which preceded it shows that the latter sees no grounds for hope. Given the pessimism of the rest of the novel, it seems probable that Alain is yet again the victim of self-deception. Laurent Mailhot sums him up in terms which show clearly his relationship to a Sartrean character (132). 'Le jeune médecin est un cocu masochiste, lucidement naïf...Il se noiera dans sa propre source visqueuse.' His hope is based on an illusion. He will remain a despised outsider who has returned to the scene of his defeat, a survenant who did not know when it was time to leave for good, a view which is not accepted by Pierre Hébert (69). 'Alain, celui qui choisit la vie et le combat, clôt le récit selon un mode actif. C'est l'homme dominé qui devient l'homme dominant.' There seems to be little evidence for this argument in the book, where the narrative supports the view of Paul Socken (175). 'It is clear that Alain's final "declaration" that he will have the townspeople love him is a momentary gesture not in keeping with his character and hence doomed to failure.' As Gilles Marcotte has said, Macklin is not to be won over by the weapons of the weak, and Alain Dubois has no other weapons (58).

Macklin, non plus que Madeleine, ne se laissera vaincre par cette arme de faible. Ce n'est pas la pitié, c'est l'amour qui est fort, et qui abat les murailles.

Le Libraire; Gérard Bessette

A few years after Langevin wrote *Poussière sur la ville* Gérard Bessette published *Le Libraire* which shares some of its features. It too is set in a small town in Quebec, Saint-Joachin, to which comes Hervé Jodoin, who is, as Jacques Allard was probably the first to say, a survenant (1970, 62). Jodoin is an educated, unemployed teacher from Montreal, who brings new ideas into the community and is able to challenge the monopoly of opinion held by the clergy. The book is set in the Duplessis years, probably in 1946, according to the calculations of Raoul (171) who follows Robidoux, when little in the town has changed from 1936, the date on the map which Jodoin borrows to find his way around. (1936 was the year when Duplessis was first elected prime minister of the province.) Piccione shows clearly how the novel symbolises the condition of the Quebec male during the Duplessis years. Even the tavern, apparently the one place to which Jodoin could escape, is not what it seems. Instead of being a centre of ideas and revolt, as the cafés had been in France before the Revolution, the taverns are places for escape and resignation where solitary drinking and lack of communication leave the Québécois stuck in the status quo (1993, 194-95). *Le Libraire* is presented by a first-person narrator who, in this case, writes a diary to record the events of his time in Saint-Joachin as there is nothing else to do to pass the time. Jodoin himself says:'Il s'agit de tuer le temps.' (11) Raoul points out that he is 'retreating into a state of limbo' (171), determined to forget the past and uninterested in the future. Where Bessette differs from Langevin, however, and indeed from Guèvremont, is that he introduces humour and satire into the genre, as Robidoux and Réjean point out (104). 'La satire s'allie au roman des mœurs dans *Le Libraire*.'[3] Guèvremont describes a year in the life of

---

[3] Once the book had been translated into English by Glen Shortliffe, it was hailed with enthusiasm by several anglophone Canadian reviewers for its satirical qualities. John Marshall, 'A Satire set in Quebec', *The Windsor Star*, February, 20, 1962. 'This is lovely satire...There is just enough cynicism to give it bite...Our French-speaking countrymen are producing some fine literature. We know of no Canadian, in the English language who can equal Bessette at the difficult art of satire.' Dorothy Bishop, 'A Novel of the Week', *The Ottawa Journal*, February 10, 1962. 'It is a fine dry book, balancing itself on a particular satiric edge that, in my recollection, has rarely been tried much less achieved in English-speaking Canada.' The reception in French Canada was much more mixed. Glen Shortliffe, 'Evolution of a Novelist:

a rural community in a remote part of Quebec, whose peaceful routine is disturbed by the arrival of the Survenant, and any humour is incidental, whereas Langevin emphasises the tragedy that results from the clash between the self-questioning incomer and the conservative, suspicious small-town dwellers of Macklin. Bessette brings out the comedy that can result from the encounter between a cynical, intelligent Montréalais and the hypocritical, narrow-minded townspeople of Saint-Joachin. As Lise Lapierre says, it is the incongruity which brings laughter (25). Bessette's aim is clearly to satirise the domination of the church in small-town Quebec under the Duplessis government, although, as Gilles Marcotte points out, the satire is not too bitter (169).

> La satire anticléricale, dans...*Le Libraire* de Gérard Bessette, ne dépasse pas les bornes de la 'bonne blague'.

That was not the opinion at the time, however, as initially Bessette could not find a publisher in Quebec and had to turn to Paris. It was only after the death of Duplessis in 1959 that it became possible to find a publisher in Quebec, as William French established (15).

The clergy are not only the target of Bessette's satire, however. The small-town mentality of 'what will people say', already seen in Guèvremont (for example, when the Survenant fights Odilon Provençal and the first thought of Alphonsine is the reaction of the parish's leading citizen, 'Quoi c'est que Pierre-Côme Provençal va penser?' (97)) is shown in both its comic and its unpleasant aspects. Lapierre points out that there are plenty of signs in the text to alert the reader to the presence of irony. Jodoin frequently records the direct speech of others to make fun of them, and his use of inverted commas almost invariably draws attention to his ironic tone. His employer, Léon Chicoine, is one of his principal targets for his sententious and over-elaborate phrases (27-29). Jodoin is indifferent to what people say about him behind his back, whereas his landlady, Rose, has experienced the full nastiness of malicious gossip and still lives in fear of its recurrence. Jodoin is also able to make fun of the Montreal officials like Martin Nault who actually finds him the job because they had been at school together. He trades on his reputation from school as a wit and a cynic to keep Martin Nault at a distance, turning

---

Gérard Bessette', *Queen's Quarterly*, 74, 1967, 41-43, gives a brief summary of the conflicting reactions.

the conversation into a highly comical farce, as Allard shows (57). Martin Nault has no understanding of the real Jodoin who drops his mask only in the diary.

Jodoin is able to treat the people of the town with indifference because he genuinely does not care about them, what they think of him or what disturbs them. As an incomer, he has no roots in the town and is unconcerned as to whether he stays or not. He has established a routine which suits him but his only interest is to be bothered as little as possible. Any form of involvement is anathema to him, as he creates, according to Allard, 'un lieu silencieux par excellence' (52-53). For Rose it is quite different, as her roots are in the town and she would find it painful to move elsewhere to make her living. The care which she takes to avoid giving offence or grounds for gossip to the locality half-amuses, half-irritates Jodoin, but the reader can understand that the problem for Rose is a very real one. Falardeau sums up the situation in Saint-Joachin very well (126).

> Dans le Saint-Joachin où habite pendant un temps *le libraire* énigmatique de Gérard Bessette, nous faisons l'apprentissage, par les allusions discrètes qui la provoquent et les implacables conséquences qu'elle entraîne, de la force du qu'en dira-t-on dans une petite ville. La vérité est ce que dit celui qui jouit auprès de ses concitoyens d'une excellente réputation. La norme qui retient d'agir selon son gré est que "ça ferait jaser les gens". Quiconque est victime de la moindre réprobation a peur de se montrer dans la rue.

Jodoin is a fair enough narrator to give Rose a voice which, however confusedly, explains her distress during the period after she had separated from her husband, a move which was not well received by the town. As Lapierre shows, however, Rose's use of language betrays her. Not only is her use of French careless, but her language reveals her *mauvaise foi*. Her claims to objectivity are denied by the violence of her denunciation of her husband (30). The result of the separation was that she had to make her peace with the Curé and thereafter take care to observe regularly all the religious requirements which would keep the gossips at bay and the Curé on her side.

The power of the church is shown by the determination of Rose to remain on the right side of the Curé even when she is conducting a secret affair with Jodoin. The lengths to which she goes to disguise the fact that they are going to the cinema together, when he asks her out, are comic in their elaboration but they betray a real fear that her behaviour would be seen and give rise to a fresh scandal. She tells

Jodoin that people would talk. 'Seulement, vous savez ce que c'est, dans une petite ville, ça ferait jaser les gens...' (82) As a result he has to agree to the farcical behaviour that they pretend to meet by chance in the cinema, sit together but leave separately so as to meet again by chance in the foyer. Jodoin is also warned by le père Manseau, the only Joachinois for whom he feels much sympathy, about the power of the clergy, a sympathy which is seen by Shek as '...a variation on the theme of the unity of the intellectual and the workers...' (297). Allard suggests that Rose and le père Manseau are his only real contacts in Saint-Joachin, because they too are viewed askance by the town, a situation which Rose survived by enlisting the help of the Curé and Manseau by retirng into near silence (58). Raoul offers a different explanation for Jodoin's interest in Manseau (173). '...this silent and immobile old alcoholic attracts him as a narcissistic projection of what he is likely to become.' Lapierre points out that le père Manseau is the only Joachinois, indeed the only character, who is not mocked by Jodoin (31). Even so minor a character as the Montreal bookseller who buys Chicoine's books is treated with irony as he puts on an act of disparaging the books to be sold, while Martin Nault is openly mocked by Jodoin playing the fool in front of him.

The major scandal breaks, after Jodoin has sold a book on the Catholic Index of forbidden books to a pupil at the big Catholic school in the town. This uncharacteristic behaviour is prompted by a sudden feeling of sympathy for the acne-troubled schoolboy who seems to be a loner, passionate about books and thus reminds Jodoin of himself when younger, which Raoul sees as 'a potential homosexual orientation' (173). She cites as evidence the suspicions of the Curé that Jodoin is an *anormal* and the rumour that he debauches schooboys. In addition he had lost his previous job in a boys' school for 'some unexplained and embarrassing reason'. Furthermore the preciosity of Jodoin's language is a trait associated with homosexuality in Bessette's *La Bagarre*. Against this must be set the evidence of the text. Jodoin makes Rose his mistress. He has had other mistresses in the past, although he admits that he is not very interested in sex. There is no sign in the book that he feels any sexual attraction to other men although he is more at ease in their company than in that of women. At best, the verdict on Raoul's theory remains to be proven. The result of his unwonted feeling of sympathy is that he agrees to sell the boy a copy of a book by Voltaire despite the instructions of Chicoine that books from the *capharnaüm* should be sold only to safe customers, an action which is interpreted by Shek as showing his nostalgia for the time when he himself really enjoyed books, as a *dévoreur* whose intellectual curiosity was still alive (296). Louise Frappier comments on the sudden emotion displayed by Jodoin when he is entrusted with the sale of books in the *capharnaüm* which gives him for the first time in years a purpose in life. According to her his mission is to release the books so that they can be read (65). The danger of such a course of action soon becomes apparent when the schoolboy's purchase is discovered by the brothers at the school, and gradually the church tightens the net round Chicoine's shop. Rose is convinced that the only way for Jodoin to outmanoeuvre his enemies is for him to see the Curé.

> Elle affirma avec fougue que je devais, dès maintenant, songer à me défendre contre les mauvaises langues acharnées à ma perte...Il fallait que j'aille au presbytère pour expliquer à M. le Curé 'sur le long et sur le large' la vraie situation. (119)

Jodoin is not prepared to agree, however. His previous encounter with the Curé has left the Curé wondering if Jodoin is an 'anormal'.

> D'abord, je le tenais de source sûre, M. le Curé me prenait pour un faible d'esprit. (122)

He had not realised that Jodoin was amusing himself at the expense of the Curé by pretending to treat his questions with total seriousness while actually making fun of him. Jodoin's act had been so successful that the Curé had had to leave the shop without finding a satisfactory answer to any of his questions. The reader, who is admitted into Jodoin's confidence by the technique of the diary entries, can appreciate to the full the irony of the scene in which the apparently sincere, but simple salesman outwits the Curé through his superior skill in language and, without ever lying, leaves the Curé baffled and literally speechless.

> M. le Curé resta quelque temps immobile, l'air perplexe, à se gratter le menton. Deux ou trois fois il ouvrit la bouche sans émettre un son. (72)

Jodoin's tactic of offering every possible assistance in flowery, ultra-polite language while actually sidestepping the Curé's real questions is completely successful and, as Allard suggests, his victory is all the more complete because it is on ground where the Curé could expect to be unchallenged (59). 'La victoire du commis réside en ce qu'il arrive à faire ce que personne à Saint-Joachin n'a pu réussir: opposer *sa parole à la Parole.*' Nonetheless the coldness of the Curé's farewell suggests that Jodoin's impertinent remarks about his eyesight have not been misunderstood.

> Je m'empressai alors de le féliciter de jouir quand même d'une si bonne vue à un âge où la plupart des gens sont impotents. (Comme je l'ai dit, il a au plus une soixantaine d'années.) (73)

Quite apart from his own distaste for religion, Jodoin realises that, after such an exchange, he is unlikely to get much help from that quarter.

Through Rose, Jodoin discovers that the town is split more than he had realised. Rose warns him that there is a clique in the town dedicated to getting Jodoin sacked and thereby forced to leave town. It is the same clique as the one which had previously singled Rose out as the target of its gossip. Jodoin's employer, Léon Chicoine, seems to be a member of the clique, and Rose warns Jodoin that Chicoine is too powerful for the Curé to attack him openly even though the two men dislike each other. This is another example of the frictions within the apparently united front of the religious element in the town. Chicoine had given Jodoin the impression that he was in awe of the power of the Curé as he was terrified after the visit of the Curé to his shop. The most profitable part of his trade was the sale of the *objets de piété* and without the approval of the Curé that trade would vanish. Rose's vivid account of the unpleasant and hypocritical nature of Chicoine serves to confirm Jodoin's growing understanding of the man who is his employer and whom he had originally thought to be '*assez bon diable*' (28). Jodoin, who is no hypocrite himself, had been convinced originally that the secret trade in forbidden books was for the principle of liberty of conscience. As he comes to realise that Chicoine is motivated by greed, his contempt for him grows. The attack on Chicoine by Rose who accuses him of being a bully ready to persecute a woman left on her own by an unsatisfactory husband adds another facet to an unpleasant character.

Chicoine himself explains to Jodoin the further divisions within the ranks of the church which are one of the reasons why the Curé is pursuing so energetically his search for the seller of the forbidden book. There is a long-running feud between the Curé and the religious order which established the school, but the feud is not doctrinal. It too involves money. The brothers responsible for the school had built a chapel which seemed too large for their needs to the Curé but he had accepted their explanations. Soon, however, a gifted preacher was drawing away from the Curé some of his parishioners with the result that his income had fallen markedly. There was, as a result, a state of undeclared war between the Curé and the brothers who were delighted to have a weapon with which to attack the Curé for lax supervision of his parish. If it could be proved that the book came from the shop of Chicoine, a leading layman in the town and the main vendor of religious items, whose shop was almost next door to the presbytery, the brothers would have a powerful weapon to discredit the Curé. Jodoin, therefore, finds himself caught between the warring parties in a feud, in which no-one is in the least interested in helping him. Chicoine's aim is to get rid of Jodoin and put all the blame on him. Rose warns Jodoin. 'Léon Chicoine ne demandait pas mieux que de se servir de moi comme bouc émissaire.' (119) The lack of charity or indeed of any religious feeling in the conflict is all the more shocking given the status of the people involved.

The hypocrisy of Chicoine had already been indicated in an earlier conversation between Jodoin and Chicoine. After his successful encounter with the Curé, Jodoin uncharacteristically found himself in a state of some excitement, partly from a childish pleasure in having outwitted the other man. When he finds himself alone in the shop with Chicoine after the other assistants have gone home, he feels a need to break the silence which for once he finds embarrassing. He asks Chicoine if there is a brothel in Saint-Joachin and finds this respectable married man with a large family surprisingly well-informed on the subject. Still posing as a liberal, Chicoine tells him that a flourishing brothel had had to close as a result of pressure from some of the townspeople. He has a friend, however, who goes regularly to the brothel in Saint-Jules who would be delighted to take Jodoin. Chicoine tries to steer a difficult course between *la liberté individuelle* and *la liberté collective* and is delighted with Jodoin's reply which Jodoin thinks he may be recalling from his readings of Rousseau.

> Je le rassurai sur ce point en lui faisant toutefois observer que ces deux sortes de liberté s'opposaient souvent; que, dans bien des cas, les individus, dont la majorité, fatalement, exprimait l'opinion générale "officielle" étaient tellement tiraillés, ballottés par des craintes, par "certaines pressions" selon son expression, que leur prétendue liberté collective était le résultat de leurs servitudes individuelles. (77)

Jodoin, who is well-read, has provided Chicoine with the intellectual justification for his position which he was unable to do for himself.

Jodoin has known from the start that his arrival in the town was unwelcome to some. Chicoine had employed him on the recommendation of Martin Nault, ignoring for whatever reason the claims of the brother of one of his employees, Mademoiselle Galarneau. She therefore treats Jodoin with hostility from the outset. He refuses to respond by allying himself with Mademoiselle Placide, her enemy. Spurned, Mademoiselle Placide becomes his enemy. Jodoin can, however, live with this hostility as long as they do not bother him. His indifference is his greatest defence against the small feuds and petty quarrels which surround him. He even tries to tell Rose that he has nothing to fear from the slanderous tongues of Saint-Joachin, as long as he is allowed to go and drink undisturbed at *Chez Trefflé*, his favourite bar, the name of which has, according to Piccione (1993, 194), associations with *noirceur* and *trou* so that it becomes both a place associated with evil and a place where the Quebec male can return to the womb, escaping the reality of his subservience to another race. He is surprised to discover from Rose that he is regarded in the town as an alcoholic and that his drinking is simply another weapon to be used against him. Nonetheless, he is quite able to withstand the pressures in a way that neither Rose nor Chicoine can. As an outsider, he has no interest in the quarrels of the Joachinois, and as he has no ambitions, he has nothing to lose. He does not need or want the friendship or support of these people, and as a consequence their power to harm him is much less than the power of the people of Macklin, for example, to harm the Dubois.

Rootless and without family or emotional ties, Jodoin comes to Saint-Joachin very much in the tradition of the survenant. He goes to Saint-Joachin simply because that is where there is an undemanding job available and because, as Shek points out, Martin Nault, who remembers that Jodoin loves books, can get him a job there (296). Jodoin does not care where the job is. He is not even sure that he would have turned the job down if he had known that Nault and Chicoine were old friends and that Nault had lent Chicoine a lot of money during a period of financial diffculties, but, as he says, speculation is useless. He took the job and, to start with, is not too dissatisfied. The work is not difficult, and he is able to establish a routine which suits him. To occupy himself when not at work he keeps his diary which becomes the channel through which Jodoin, and behind him Bessette, can show how he gradually becomes aware of the hypocrisy and feuding behind the mask of conventional respectability put forward by the people of Saint-Joachin. Mailhot compares Bessette to Camus in the effectiveness of his sparse style (155-56). The churchmen are feuding for reasons which are far from religious, but very much of this world. The leading laymen in the town, represented by Chicoine are shown to be blatant liars and hypocrites. The denunciations of Rose could be written off as the aftermath of small-town feuding but Jodoin gradually realises that Chicoine's unscrupulous behaviour confirms everything that she says, although he cannot prove, of course, that Chicoine did try to proposition her after she had left her husband. It would be consistent with his character, however, to try to take advantage of someone weaker. When the scandal becomes so great that his business is threatened, Chicoine is more than ready to sacrifice Jodoin who has served him loyally and tried to protect him from the enquiries of the Curé. Chicoine disgusts Jodoin by the hypocrisy with which he tries to involve him in the scheme which he has hatched.

> M. Chicoine s'approcha alors de moi...et d'une voix excitée qui butait sur les syllabes, il se mit à m'exposer son plan. Tout d'abord je crus que j'avais mal compris. Ses vantardises précédentes, ses expressions pugnaces avaient évoqué à mon esprit une expédition audacieuse, spectaculaire. Au lieu de cela, que me proposait-il? - Une vulgaire petite combine, comme honteuse de soi, qui avait tous les caractères d'une effraction. Je me rendis compte alors que, malgré toutes ses pompeuses déclarations, Léon Chicoine n'était qu'un pauvre type foirant de peur qui songeait à protéger à tout prix son petit commerce. (140-41)

The liberal principles which were evoked to persuade Jodoin to assist Chicoine in his under-the-counter trade count for nothing when Chicoine sees his profits about to shrink or disappear. The complaints of Rose show the wretched position of unprotected women in a town where men dominated. Once separated from her husband she is vulnerable to pressure from the likes of Chicoine and has to put up with the groping of her elderly employer to keep the job which she needs now that she has no husband.

Saint-Joachin is seriously affected by the brief stay of Jodoin. He stays for less than three months, but by the time of his return to Montreal, Saint-Joachin has had its mask of respectability torn away. The quarrels between the two branches of the Catholic church have been brought into the open. The whole town is aware of the financial motives which lie behind these quarrels. The hypocrisy and immorality of some of the Saint-Joachinois have been exposed to Jodoin's cynical gaze. The fear of spiteful gossip has been shown to dominate the lives of most people forcing them to conform to the requirements of the church, at least superficially.

Jodoin has brought a little excitement into the life of Rose whose lover he briefly became. He has seriously destabilised the business of Chicoine who will probably have to abandon his trade in books so as to rebuild his links with the church. Jodoin has also cheated Chicoine out of a considerable sum by appropriating the forbidden books and selling them for his own gain in the full knowledge that Chicoine dare not pursue him. The Curé and the brothers who run the school have not only had to try to cope with an incident which challenged their authority both in the school and in the town but they have lost face. They have been made to look ridiculous by their reaction to an incident which hardly deserved the attention and excitement which it generated. A schoolboy reading a forbidden book sets the whole town by the ears. The Catholic Church is made to look petty as well as interfering and lacking in Christian charity. The respectable citizens of Saint-Joachin are shown to be frauds and dishonest. Jodoin's calm narrative draws the reader into sympathising with him so that at the end of the book his theft of the books seems a richly deserved punishment for Léon Chicoine. The reader can see that it is a case of the biter bit and joins with Jodoin in enjoying his little triumph at the expense of the hypocritical provincial. Jodoin's role has changed from that of spectator and commentator to actor.

Bessette uses the figure of the survenant to expose the stifling conformity and the hypocrisy of provincial life in Quebec under the Duplessis government when the Catholic church was still extremely powerful. Shek attributes Bessette's pessimism to this period (300). 'Gérard Bessette's *L'Incubation* is a work of pessimistic humanism, probably marked, as was *Le Libraire*, by the author's scars received during the dark Duplessis years...' His satire is anti-clerical and is perhaps more biting than Gilles Marcotte suggested. There is nothing sympathetic or admirable about the clergy in *Le Libraire*. They are exposed as men with many flaws and far from united amongst themselves. Small-town life is damned through the eyes of a lazy, cynical intellectual with a sharp tongue and a clear mind, distanced from the town by his status as an incomer, by his attachment to alcohol and his indifference to religion. The importance of alcohol in estranging him from the town is underlined by Cronin (202). '...l'alcool crée une *distance* entre les personnages du roman et les normes sociales.' Thanks to his honesty and to the self-awareness which he shows, describing his appearance and his motives with a brutal realism, for example, Jodoin is able to keep the reader on his side. The power of his words is such that he can make the reader forget that this account is his side of the story, as Jacques Allard has shown (55). 'En effet, quand il décide de "gratter du papier" plutôt que de "lever le coude", il écrit mais n'écrit pas tout.' His apparent honesty and lucidity are attractive when compared with the hypocrisy and self-deception of almost every other character in the book. Robidoux and Réjean bring out very well the contrasting sides of Jodoin's character (111).

> Il est sans scrupule, mais il peut être digne et fier en même temps: ainsi accepte-t-il, moyennant le prix, de dépanner Chicoine, mais refuse de lui serrer la main. Et malgré le sale coup qu'il joue à son employeur, qui le mérite bien, il est suffisamment honnête pour mettre le lecteur de son côté.

Piccione brings out the contrast between him and the Joachinois who are incapable of comprehending the ideas to which Jodoin refers. Where he talks about liberty of conscience with Chicoine and is even moved by such an ideal, their hope is that he will be able to supply them with some pornography. This brief scene illustrates the difference between the intellectual levels of Jodoin and the provincial Québécois whom he despises and makes it clear that Bessette is inviting the reader to join Jodoin in his contempt (Piccione, 194-95). Even the fact that Jodoin writes in a precious, self-consciously correct French, laughing unkindly at those, like Rose, who speak incorrectly, laughter which is designed to boost his self-esteem, does not alienate the reader. As Raoul comments, the diary form enables Jodoin to listen to himself rather than to communicate with anyone else (175). By creating such an original and entertaining character who exposes the stifling atmosphere of Quebec during the rule of Maurice Duplessis, Bessette has given a fresh and entertaining twist to a theme which continues to be closely linked to Quebec traditions. As Piccione makes clear, the whole book is a scathing indictment of Quebec society during the Duplessis years, very much in tune with the atitudes of *Parti Pris* and the intellectuals associated with it (passim). In Bessette's hands the survenant becomes a vehicle by which a corrupt and reactionary provincial government can be attacked with humour and satire.

Les Fous de Bassan; Anne Hébert

Whereas Guèvremont, Langevin and Bessette have all shown the effect of the arrival of a total stranger in a community which rejected him to a greater or less extent and survived, however damaged, the upset of his incursion, Anne Hébert gives a new slant to the genre in *Les Fous de Bassan*. She chooses as her setting the anglophone village of Griffin Creek (a name chosen, no doubt, for its symbolic attachment to evil as Antoine Sirois suggests (134): '...Griffon Creek, nom significatif, puisque le griffon, dans la symbolique chrétienne, est l'image du démon') on the Saint Lawrence, which had been settled in the eighteenth century by four Loyalist families from Vermont. They had turned this remote and inhospitable region into a prosperous farming and fishing community, intermarried and produced numerous children. By 1936 the outside world has still not really impinged on their isolated existence, but after that summer the community would never be the same. Part of the narrative is set in 1982 when it has shrunk to a few elderly survivors whose leader is the octogenarian pastor, Nicolas Jones. By dividing the narrative between six different narrators (Nicolas Jones, Stevens Brown twice, his cousins Nora and Olivia Atkins, his brother Perceval and *autres voix*) and two time periods, Hébert can examine the events of the summer of 1936 which saw the arrival and departure of her survenant and the aftermath which shows the community on the edge of extinction as a result of the conflicts generated by the summer of 1936.

The survenant is Stevens Brown, a young man who has spent the past five years bumming around the United States and at the age of twenty decides to return briefly to his native village on the shores of the Saint Lawrence. Kelton Knight interprets this return as a desire to reposition himself in life (103).

> In addition, Stevens' return 'au bercail' seems pushed by the necessity to reevaluate his childhood from the point of view of his manhood and to reassure himself that the blood now flowing in his veins is not the same as it was when he left.

Later in his book Knight argues that the return of Stevens is also motivated by his desire to associate himself with the innocence of the simple-minded Perceval (107).

> ...Stevens's return to Griffin Creek is motivated by his brother Perceval. For Stevens, Perceval's unsullied soul is a pathway where is [sic] left the footprints of his own blameless childhood, a prerequisite to knowing who he is, or, at least, whom [sic] he wants to be, and a necessary condition for his break with the past.'

Scott Lee takes this interpretation even further (379).

> Ce qui motive le retour de Stevens Brown à son village natal de Griffin Creek paraît être une volonté non de retrouver une enfance perdue, mais de recommencer à zéro.

Plausible as these interpretations are, there is no explicit textual evidence for them, and once Stevens is back in the village, it becomes clear that he is driven by a need to exorcise the demons of his childhood, as Côté and Mitchell suggest (81). He is so altered that, at first, he is recognised only with difficulty and, in the course of five years, the children have forgotten about him and regard him as a stranger. Five years in the USA have left him eager to see his birthplace again, although he is quite clear in his own mind that his stay will be brief. Indeed, if he is not recognised, he intends to leave immediately. As Andrée Stephan suggests, Stevens is like the migrating birds which nest around Griffin Creek (118).

> Or Stevens est lui aussi un migrateur: il a quitté son village pour gagner les rivages lumineux de Floride et il n'est rentré que pour repartir.

Lucie Guillemette points out that this similarity is not unnoticed by the characters in the book, as Perceval the fool, who sees more than he can express, sees his brother as a migratory bird in search of sun and warmth (346).

> En comparant son frère au fou de Bassan, l'adolescent retardé perçoit Stevens comme un être en migration que les déplacements intermittents conduisent vers les terres de soleil et de chaleur.

Once reestablished in the village and working for his cousin, Maureen Macdonald, Stevens never deviates from his plan to go back to Florida in the autumn, leaving behind the people and the place for which he feels little affection. It is clear, although never explicitly stated, that one of his reasons for returning is to triumph over his parents by showing that he has survived without them and that he is no longer under their authority. There is no family affection in his attitude. He feels nothing for his parents except intense dislike and resentment for the cruelty with which they brought him up. Côté and Mitchell show quite clearly how Hébert is reworking the Œdipus myth, as she did in *Le Torrent*, with her emphasis on the damage done to the male child by uncaring and cruel parents (80). He has little affection for his numerous other relatives either, although he does care for his siblings, particularly the feeble-minded Perceval, his brother, with whom he identifies. One of his fantasies is to rescue his brother together with their twin sisters and to carry them off with him to Florida where they will be far away from the brutality and coldness of their father and mother. This is a clear reference to fairy tale, for, as Frédérique Chevillot points out, Anne Hébert draws on the Pied Piper story, in which the children leave their parents, and Hop o' my Thumb, in which the children are abandoned by their parents, to significant effect in *Les Fous de Bassan* (127). As Reid realises, however, Stevens has no intention of translating such a dream into reality. He does not envisage his future life encumbered by feeble-minded siblings (121).

> The only real human contact that Stevens has is a kind of hopeless affection for the twins and Perceval, which Stevens is too worldly-wise to nurture. Stevens's ensuing crisis of identity is only natural in such extreme isolation.

For the other inhabitants of Griffin Creek, apart from his grandmother, the only person for whom he would lift his hat, he feels contempt and loathing. When he does finally revisit his parents, he is dressed formally in the suit of the dead husband of his mistress, and the three of them sit formally in the parlour, through the open door of which he can see the exact spot where he and his father fought violently on the floor of the kitchen five years before. Already at fifteen he was strong enough to hold his father to a drawn battle. At twenty, after five years of wandering and physical labour, he is the stronger and he enjoys the older man's tacit acceptance of his dominance. Only after the disappearance of his cousins, Nora and Olivia, does he move back into the house of his parents, as it is necessary to present a united front to the new intruders, the police. The whole village temporarily closes ranks against the common enemy, but nonetheless the police arrest Stevens and remove him from the village to which he never returns. His final letter, dated 1982, is from Montreal where he has escaped from the hospital for Second World-War casualties and taken refuge in a small room on the

Côte des Neiges. There he tries to exorcise the demons of the past, symbolised by the gannets which seem to be dive-bombing his skull with piercing shrieks, as he explains in the letter to his friend in Florida, Old Mic, a letter which may never be sent. If it is sent, it may never be read, as Stevens does not know if Mic is still alive. Frédérique Chevillot suggests plausibly that the letters are a device on the part of Stevens to provide himself with an audience, an audience which, he admits, never replies (125).

> Stevens - le seul peut-être à se savoir fou - écrit des lettres à "un destinataire qui ne répond jamais" (82). Redoutant de n'écrire que pour lui-même Stevens prétend écrire à un autre.

The readers, however, are finally admitted to the secret of what happened on the night of August 31st, 1936, as Stevens confesses to the murder of his cousins, Nora and Olivia, and the rape of Olivia. A question-mark remains in the mind of the reader, however, for their uncle, Nicolas Jones, was also on the beach where the murders took place that night, as was Perceval. The clear sense of guilt experienced by Nicolas may, as Côté and Mitchell suggest, be due to the fact that he was a witness to the murders and the rape and did nothing to prevent them (89, note 6). Also the author leaves unclear just how far the recollections of a war veteran, doped to the eyeballs with sedatives and tranquillisers, whose mental condition has kept him in hospital for thirty-six years, can be trusted.

The return of Stevens disrupts the life of everyone in the village. He himself looks down on it on the first morning, cold-bloodedly deciding which of the houses he will visit first. As everyone in the village is related to everyone else, he has a claim on all of them. Although tempted to throw himself at the feet of his grandmother, the matriarch of the village, and seek her absolution, he resists the idea and goes instead to the house of Maureen Macdonald, his widowed cousin approaching fifty, whose hired man he becomes for the rest of the summer. Stevens has already let the reader know that he is very attractive to the opposite sex. On his journey north from Florida he has kept the women at bay only by working as a fishgutter so that the smell discouraged them. Even when covered in dust and mud, he is so attractive that Maureen is overcome with weakness at the sight of him naked in the bath, and he has no trouble in seducing her. Briefly she enjoys an Indian summer of sexual pleasure. Her cousins notice that she is using make-up and taking great care over her hair. Stevens humours her when he is in the mood by making love to her, but refuses to move into the house and share her bed. He insists on preserving appearances by sleeping in the hayloft like any other hired man, where he can be free of the overcloying attention of Maureen and masturbate in peace. For Stevens, Maureen is a source of income, useful because she provides a place to stay, but a nuisance because she becomes too demanding and too serious about him. In fact, Maureen, who is the same generation as Steven's mother, is the victim of his ill-treatment which culminates in him telling her that she is old. Through her he is taking revenge on the other woman whose coldness and indifference have left him damaged forever and hostile to all women, as Reid comments (122). 'Maureen's solitude is Stevens's vengeance against woman-kind. His alienation grows, his bitterness heightens.' As Lucie Guillemette suggests, his return to his native village unleashes the full force of his misogyny (346).

> Or la misogynie déclarée du personnage...atteint son paroxysme dans le climat conventionnel de son village natal que l'étroitesse des lieux rend d'autant plus rigide.

Maureen is shattered by his rejection and even more by the news of the death of her two young cousins. They had been at her house until 9:30 that night and had left to go home but instead had gone down to the beach where they met their deaths. Stevens's stay at Griffin Creek destroyed Maureen's peace of mind. Before he came, she was living peacefully as a widow, running her small-holding and living an apparently contented life. The irruption of the attractive young man into her quiet existence reawakens her sexually and for a moment renews her youth, but almost immediately she sees herself rejected for her younger cousins and is left disappointed and disillusioned - dismissed in the most wounding way possible. She does not realise, as Patricia Louette suggests, that for Stevens she has acted as a mother-substitute, an object on which he can vent the hatred that he feels for his mother (318).

> Elle [Maureen] attire Stevens parce qu'elle incarne sa mère Bea. A travers son amante, c'est sa méchante mère qu'il atteint. Le réveil sensuel de la "vieille" Maureen le renvoie à l'activité sexuelle de Bea (qui rêve de se retrouver seule avec son mari, sans enfant).

By the start of September she is looking and acting much older than her years, barely able to control herself as she struggles with the terrible questions that obviously haunt her after the deaths of Nora and Olivia.

The return of Stevens also has a disastrous effect on Perceval, the only being for whom he cares. Perceval adores Stevens who treats him with a rather casual affection but is never cruel to him unlike their cold and brutal parents who regularly beat Perceval and lock him up in his room. The return of Stevens is very exciting for Perceval as 'Stevens est bon pour moi' (142). Perceval is fifteen and growing into a huge adolescent gradually becoming aware of his own sexuality. His attempts to grope his pretty cousin, Nora, on the beach lead to a serious beating from his father when the truth is revealed by Felicity, the grandmother of both teenagers. Perceval is almost as interested in Nora and Olivia as Stevens, and after their death his decline is rapid. He is haunted by their images, seeing them dancing in the sunlight where the sky meets the sea, only for the vision to fade as they return to their natural elements for both Nora and Olivia in different ways are identified with the sea. He takes part in the search for them on the night of their disappearance, revelling in being able to join in the shouting as much as he wants. He knows more than he is able or willing to reveal and eavesdrops anxiously on the interrogations of Stevens by the unpleasant policeman, McKenna. McKenna, who is not a fool, realises that Perceval might be able to give him information that would be useful, but Perceval is practised in pretending to be stupider than he is and gives nothing away. He watches with interest as his father destroys some of the evidence that comes ashore, burning the pink belt that had been Nora's. The excitement makes him more than usually irritating for his parents. The other men on the search find his shouting and nervous excitement troublesome and he is sent home to be locked in his room. The fact that he is growing too big to control physically is noted. His unhappiness after the arrest of Stevens makes him more difficiult still and his parents have no hesitation in sending him away to the asylum where he will spend the rest of his days, longing for the affection that no one except Stevens and the twins bothered to show him. With Stevens gone there is no one to control him. He might have been able to live in Florida with Stevens but in Griffin Creek his parents are only too eager to be rid of him. The events of the summer worsen his fragile mental state which gives them their excuse. Perceval, the innocent fool, has to spend the rest of his life atoning for the sins of others.

The events of the summer also settle the fate of the twins, Pam and Pat, the sisters of Stevens and Perceval. Their role in the story of Stevens is minimal, although he realises that they, like their brothers, are the unloved offspring of Bea and John Atkins. They are dispatched to the parsonage to keep house for the Reverend Nicolas Jones, now a widower after the suicide of his wife, Irene Jones. Sent there as young teenagers, they are still there in 1982, ageing, losing their femininity and tyrannised by the pastor who loves to intimidate and criticise them. He is shocked to discover that they still have the strength to defy him and sabotage his great project. Lacking any heir because Irene was barren, Nicolas Jones decides to recreate his ancestors by painting *'une galerie des ancêtres'* (14) in the annexe which he has added to the parsonage. He is responsible for painting his male ancestors and entrusts the painting of the female ancestors to the twins, only to discover to his fury that they use the features of the dead Nora, Olivia and Irene and that they paint as a scroll the word *été* and the figures *1936* right round the wall. Suddenly he realises that these women whom he despises are haunted by the events of thirty odd years ago. They are not the ciphers that he had thought. They have their own independent, secret thoughts and shared confidences from which he is excluded. They bring back to his mind the recollection of the events of 1936 from which he shrinks, realising that he had his share of the guilt in them. The twins reactivate his conscience and, although he blames Stevens for being the most evil member of the doomed community of Griffin Creek, he is aware that he too was a sinner. Ghostlike creatures on the margin of the story, the twins never knew the joys of childhood and adolesence because of the indifference of their parents and are dwindling into old age without ever experiencing life as women. The upset caused by the crimes of Stevens gave their parents the opportunity to get rid of them, and the tyrannical rule of the pastor has kept them secluded ever since.

The characters most affected by the return of Stevens are the two Atkins cousins, Nora and Olivia. Although they have been linked together like Siamese twins throughout their lives despite the difference of two years in their age, their growing sexual awareness drives them apart after the return of Stevens to whom they are both instantly attracted, as Bishop points out (1993, 221). '...le désir que Nora et Olivia éprouvaient pour Stevens Brown les éloigne/exile l'une de l'autre.' Nora, the younger of the two at fifteen, is just becoming aware of her power of attraction over men. She is quite deliberately experimenting with her sexuality, hoping that by the end of the summer she will have kissed all the available young men. Further than that she does not intend to go since, as Stevens recognises, the girls of the village are sacrosanct until they marry which is why he goes with his cousin, Patrick, and Bob Allen to the brothels along the coast. Nonetheless she is powerfully attracted to Stevens, partly because he is new and therefore different from the other boys. She does not remember him very well as she was only ten when he left the village. She is also very aware of his attractiveness to women. She pursues him into the forest tracking him like a huntress until the moment when he turns to confront her. Suddenly her strength deserts her, and to her fury she realises that she is now the prey and he the hunter, a possible prefiguraton of the scene on the beach where Stevens rapes and strangles her, according to Côté and Mitchell (83). Her fury is increased by the attitude of Stevens who shows an amused lack of interest in her, leaning against a tree trunk, hands in pockets and looking as if at any moment he is about to start whistling. He is sufficiently uninterested and self-controlled not to take advantage of her, although she has put herself in his power. He warns her not to do anything that she might regret. Insulted by his lack of interest she runs from him, and his rebuff drives her into the arms of her uncle Nicolas who, as she is perfectly aware, has been showing an unhealthy interest in her all summer. To revenge herself on Stevens, Nora calmly allows Nicolas to fondle and grope her in the boathouse, despite her wish that he not be the first to initiate her into sex. They are seen by Perceval, also strongly attracted to Nora, who runs off to tell Irene. She has no difficulty in understanding his unhappy babblings, but utters almost no reproach to her husband. Instead she quietly purchases a strong rope from the store and in the course of the night hangs herself, leaving Nicolas to feel guilty and aware of his sin for the rest of his life. There is a direct chain of cause and effect between Stevens's rejection of Nora in the forest to the death of Irene, who is the first victim of Stevens's return to Griffin Creek.

Nora is acutely aware that Stevens is more attracted to Olivia than he is to her. The cousins have become sexual rivals, and Nora, the more confident because the more loved at home, is not afraid to challenge Stevens. She jealously decries Olivia's beauty, telling Stevens that one of Olivia's feet is webbed, quite unaware that this will excite an unhealthy interest in him. He becomes fascinated by the idea of this foot and desperate to see it. Unintentionally Nora has added to the fascination which Olivia exerts on him. Nora is longing to find out about sex. She is looking forward to marriage and a large family. She dreams of escape from Griffin Creek with the prince of the land of oranges or cotton or, later, with a pirate captain who will fasten her to the prow of his ship as a figurehead. The arrival of Stevens coincides with these dreams, and it is likely that he has in part provoked them. Nora's angry disappointment is all the easier to understand if it is associated with the frustration of her dreams by this promising newcomer who turns out to be indifferent to her. She cannot understand his lack of interest when all the men she knows in the village and any visitors, like the American in his big car, are clearly attracted to her. When she takes lunch to the hunters in the forest, the interest of her cousin, Sidney, and her Uncle Nicolas is so obvious, that her father intervenes sharply to send her home before anything can develop.

The climax of the summer comes on the 31st of August, the night before Stevens's departure for Florida where he hopes to live with Old Mic. Nora and Olivia, who is staying with her uncle and aunt while her father and brothers are away on business, visit Maureen, but as they make their way home they are intercepted by Stevens who has been on the beach bailing out the boat. He takes Olivia's arm while Nora walks ahead, scorning him, and the three of them descend to the beach. There Nora turns on him screaming the foulest abuse in the language of the men of Griffin Creek. Laughing and crying hysterically she accuses him of unmanliness, and when Olivia tries to calm her, she warns Olivia against Stevens, repeating the insult. Does she sense that Stevens is not committed to heterosexuality? His relationship with Old Mic is ambiguous but could well be homosexual. His contempt for and indifference to women have been manifest on several occasions, as in the way he treats Maureen, or the trouble he takes to make himself less attractive to women as he journeys north back to Griffin Creek. His resentment against and dislike of women are openly voiced in his letter to Old Mic. His cold and unloving mother has alienated him forever from her sex. Knight sees the violence of Stevens as a reflection of his inability to hurt his mother. Instead, he turns his hostility to her on to the other women of the village (105).

> The process of self-delusion continues as he sets out to punish his mother. Unable to project his anger directly upon her, he spits his vitriol at the faces of his cousins, Maureen, Nora and Olivia, thinking that elements of his mother are to be found in all women.

Whatever Nora guesses about Stevens, her laughter is the cause of her death. Stevens puts his hand on her throat to try to quieten the laughter, but Nora is so slight that the least pressure is enough to strangle her, and suddenly she is lying dead at his feet. The sight of this girl, who a moment before has been full of rage and scorn, crumpled on the sand before him, is a memory that Stevens admits gives him pleasure through all the horrors of war and long after, as he savours the joy of seeing her 'matée et domptée' (245) with all her woman's envy and contempt defeated. Nora ends her life as the victim of Stevens's misogyny, a life full of hope and promise, brutally shortened by his return to Griffin Creek. Nevertheless, she does not disappear from his life. As Lee points out, she is present in spirit in the room where Stevens awaits the end of his life (387).

> Si Nora n'est pas physiquement présente dans la chambre du vieux Stevens, elle exerce une influence non moins troublante dans l'esprit de celui-ci, lui faisant revivre ce que, par le meurtre du 31 août 1936, il croyait rendre absent.

In this way she is avenged on her murderer, who, as Voichita Sasu comments, is not punished for his crimes. His punishment comes later (178).

> Les crimes de Stevens ne sont pas punis par la loi humaine. Il est jugé et acquitté, il échappe à la guerre, 'indemne de la tête aux pieds', mais 'complètement détraqué'. Bien que tardif, le châtiment qu'il ne veut pas assumer --'C'est la guerre mon vieux, rien d'autre que les séquelles de la guerre, te dis-je, Griffin Creek n'y est pour rien' (p.232), --s'appesantira sur son cœur 'aussi gros qu'une meule dans la poitrine', s'installera dans ses cauchemars, pointera, au réveil, au moment de 'renouer avec son horreur particulière'.

Olivia, the older cousin, is always more wary and reserved than Nora. Olivia's mother is dead, and Olivia's memories suggest that her life was not very happy. The bruises that the little girl sees suggest that her mother may have been beaten by her father. Even though she was clearly very ill, in fact dying, she still had to undertake the heavy labour of the potato harvest without the help of her men. Olivia suspects that the coarse behaviour of Patrick and Sidney, adolescents eager to become men, may have added to her mother's unhappiness. Olivia does not share the optimism of Nora who came from an apparently happy household where the mother and father were on affectionate, teasing terms and the father was not afraid to reveal his affection for his daughters to them, although he became more reserved as they approached puberty. Olivia was entrusted to the safekeeping of her father and brothers by her dying mother who made the little girl promise to be obedient. As a result she is closely guarded by three watchful males who protect their property grimly against any intruder. She feels both a prisoner and a slave as she keeps house for all three of them, and her first encounter with Stevens is, in fact, while she is ironing, with her brother, Patrick, sleeping upstairs, a fact which she hastens to let Stevens know.

Olivia is immediately aware of the threat posed by Stevens. The ancestral voices of her mother and grandmothers echo through her subconscious, warning her that this boy is evil and not to be trusted. She uses the ironing as a barrier to keep him at bay, pretending not to recognise him until the pretence cannot be kept up any longer. She knows from the outset that she must discipline herself against him, as she is all too aware of his attraction. It gradually emerges that before Stevens left, he and Olivia were already very aware of each other. As children, playing on the beach they were drawn together, Olivia longing to protect the rebellious little boy from the cruelty of his father, her Uncle John. As teenagers, Stevens took more interest in her than her brothers ever did, even allowing her occasionally to participate in the boys' games. The attraction is not new, therefore, but Olivia is no longer a trusting, little girl, and Stevens has become hard and cruel, linking Olivia with the other women who, in his eyes, overpopulate the village and on whom he seeks revenge.

> Il y a trop de femmes dans ce village, trop de femmes en chaleur...Des femmes. Toujours des femmes. Il ne s'agit plus de cette vieille Maureen ou de la petite Nora. Olivia est plus coriace, résistante dans sa peur de moi, sa peur de ce qui peut lui venir de moi, de mon corps sauvage, de mon cœur mauvais. (80)

Worse still, Olivia becomes the one against whom he is most enraged as she seeks to avoid him and keep her distance from him while he manoeuvres to attract her interest or, at least, her attention.

Stevens does not realise that he actually has all the attention that he could wish for. Olivia knows that he is temptation, that he could be for her the source of knowledge. She compares him to the tree of knowledge, and the parallels with Eve and the serpent in the Garden of Eden are clear, if implicit.

> Il est comme l'arbre planté au milieu du paradis terrestre. La science du bien et du mal n'a pas de secret pour lui. Si seulement je voulais bien, j'apprendrais tout de lui, d'un seul coup, la vie, la mort, tout. (216)

Sirois has shown that Stevens is the serpent of temptation for Olivia and Nora, both of whom are longing for sexual knowledge and to move from adolescence to womanhood. In spite, or even because, of the sinister atmosphere which surrounds him, they are drawn to him and will, in the end, meet their death through the combination of their desire and his evil (1997, 134-35).

> Le jeune homme éveille la curiosité et l'intérêt de deux adolescentes, Olivia, ...et Nora... Elles brûlent, dans leur innocence, de faire l'expérience de l'amour...Tout en connaissant le "cœur mauvais" de ce dernier [Stevens] et en dépit des mises en garde des femmes, les deux adolescentes suivront Stevens, déjà affublé, dans le récit, des noms de serpent, de tentateur, de diable d'homme, dans les ténèbres de la nuit, sur une plage isolée, pour y découvrir le viol et la mort.

Throughout the summer Olivia is determined not to reveal to him that she is attracted by him. She feels that she would die of shame if he should discover her secret.

> S'il me voyait rougir devant lui, à cause de lui qui me tourmente, une fois, une fois seulement et je mourrais de honte. (217)

Even when Stevens is roused by the sight of her swimming, mastering the mountainous waves so easily that he thinks that she is Patrick, the 'maître-nageur', and rushes to seize her on the beach, she resists him. For him she is like a mermaid whose webbed foot he longs to see, as she tries to elude him, but he is immediately interrupted by Patrick or Sidney who leaps to defend his sister, and there is a violent fight between the cousins which ends with honours more or less even. Olivia's fantasy is to wrestle on a moonlit beach with Stevens until one or the other is pinned to the ground, when at last she would be his equal. In reality, however, she has no intention of giving way to either his temptation or her own desire. At the barn dance she avoids his gaze in contrast to Nora who flaunts herself in front of him to catch his attention and then spurn him. Olivia is aware that Nora is her rival and, when she goes to stay at her aunt's while her father and brothers are away, she can no longer bear to share Nora's bed. Instead she pretends to sleep on the floor, listening to the rhythmic breathing of Nora and her sisters, while outside the storm rages. Olivia lies awake straining to hear the voice of Stevens calling to her and admitting to herself that if she did hear it she would get up and go out, against all the warnings of her ancestresses and risking the wrath of their living representative, her Aunt Alice.

Olivia meets her death almost by accident. After Stevens has killed Nora, he obviously cannot allow the only witness to escape and alert the village. Olivia has turned to flight, but quick as she is, he is quicker and tackles her to the ground where he rapes her, revelling in the defilement which he is inflicting on this girl whom he has described as too pure. Olivia has to bear the force of his hatred against all women as he treats her like a whore, giving vent to his fury and his desire to hurt which will give him revenge on his cold, unfeeling parents.

> L'injurier en paix. L'appeler salope. La démasquer, elle, la fille trop belle et trop sage. A tant faire l'ange on...Lui faire avouer qu'elle est velue, sous sa culotte, comme une bête. Le défaut caché de sa belle personne solennelle, cette touffe noire et humide entre ses cuisses là où je fornique comme chez les guidounes... (248)

As he comes to, Stevens realises that Olivia's piercing screams, like Nora's hysterical laughter, must be silenced. He has killed once, quickly and easily, and has no hesitation in using the same method again before throwing both bodies into the sea to be carried away. Just as he subsequently enjoyed the the recollection of Nora dead at his feet, he also, as Reid argues (119), enjoys the idea that through him Olivia was 'made a woman' before she died, thus implicitly disproving Nora's accusation, which sparked the dénouement of the tragedy, that he 'was not a man'.

> Stevens Brown killed his cousins because Nora charged he was "not a man" (244). Stevens's smug contention that Olivia "est devenu [sic] femme comme les autres" (239) before she died brings to the foreground his adherence to this notion that we become "men" and "women" through the rite of coitus.

Olivia has died as she lived, the victim of the men amongst whom she lived. Her father and brothers exploited her in return for their protection. Their despairing reaction to her death suggests that deep within they did feel affection for her, but, unlike Nora's father and brothers, they were unable to express it while she lived. As for Nora, the summer of 1936 is the summer when Olivia awakens to love, but whereas for Nora love is a game to be played with many players until she chooses the mate with whom she will settle down, Olivia is deeply attracted to one man from the start. She has fond memories of him, and yet, because of his absence, he is a stranger who has become very attractive and is clearly interested in her. He keeps her guessing, however, as to just how interested, for Olivia is never quite sure whether Stevens prefers her to Nora, while Nora knows that Stevens prefers Olivia. No doubt feeling that while she and Nora were together, they were both safe in the company of their cousin, Olivia, arm-in-arm with Stevens, willingly follows Nora to the beach where Nora's jealousy explodes and Olivia's fantasy of wrestling with Stevens on a moonlit beach turns into a ghastly reality of rape and murder. Victim of her own beauty, victim of the resentment of Griffin Creek men against cold, unloving mothers and grandmothers, Olivia, like Nora, has her life cut short by the return of Stevens.

Nora and Olivia are the most obvious victims of the return of Stevens to Griffin Creek, although Perceval and Maureen Macdonald suffer in different ways, and the twins are banished to a life of servitude in the house of the pastor, Nicolas Jones. The pastor himself also suffers. As has been shown, the suicide of his wife is clearly linked to the return of Stevens, although the immediate cause is the pastor's infidelity as he tries to seduce his niece. He does not actually make love to Nora, but he is potentially guilty of both adultery and incest and so is aware that Stevens is not the only cause of the evil in Griffin Creek. With hindsight in 1982 he does recognise that Stevens was the most evil of them all.

> ...j'interroge mon âme et cherche la faute originelle de Griffin Creek. Non, ce n'est pas Stevens qui a manqué le premier, quoiqu'il soit le pire de nous tous, le dépositaire de toute la malfaisance secrète de Griffin Creek, amassée au cœur des hommes et des femmes depuis deux siècles. (27)

Painfully Nicolas Jones has to admit that Griffin Creek, inbred and isolated, is steeped in evil in which he participated. He recognises that he is the brother of the other men, fierce hunters who return home with their prey and take their wives in the dark without even removing their boots. He resents bitterly the fact that his lust is fruitless as Irene is barren. However much he makes love to her, his prayers for a son who might capture the heart of Nicolas's mother, Felicity, in a way that Nicolas himself never managed, go unanswered. He has no descendants, and after the events of the summer of 1936 he has to recognise that he is the last of his line. All that he can leave behind is the picture gallery of his ancestors, which is sabotaged by the twins inserting into it the memories which he most wished to bury.

Nicolas Jones had decided at the age of ten to become a minister of religion in a bid to gain the attention and affection of his mother, who had turned against all men because of the many infidelities of her husband, Peter Jones. Briefly he succeeds, and Francoli sees this as evidence of his 'libidinal fascination with his mother' (137), in which view she is supported by Côté and Mitchell, who compare the figure of Felicity with Claudine in *Le Torrent* to show how the same theme resurfaces in the work of Hébert and how damaging the effect of a remote mother figure can be to a man like Nicolas Jones. He is supplanted in her affections by her granddaughters, Nora and Olivia, and is viewed with a cold detachment by his mother. Felicity understands all too well the lust that drives him in pursuit of Nora. She can see through the self-centredness which makes him enjoy the sound of his beautiful voice. The summer of 1936 is the point at which he loses some of his magic. Nora realises that he is no longer truly the voice of God.

> Mon oncle Nicolas parle de Dieu, pense Nora Atkins, mais depuis quelque temps je n'entends plus la parole de Dieu dans la voix de l'oncle Nicolas. C'est comme si Dieu se taisait dans la voix de l'oncle Nicolas. La voix sonore de l'oncle Nicolas, sans rien de pieux dedans, la belle voix de l'oncle Nicolas comme une écale brillante, vide de tout contenu, basse et virile, fluide comme de la fumée. (30)

Nicolas recognises that he is making special efforts to impress his niece. Nora, whose flaming red hair so closely resembles his own as Irene points out in the sole comment which alerts Nicolas to the fact that she knows what he and Nora were doing in the boathouse, interests him far more than Olivia. He is immediately aware when he loses Nora's attention in church when she turns to look at Stevens who has suddenly appeared in the church door. Stevens stands there looking at Nora until the whole church has turned to look at him and, as Nicolas realises, judge him. Then he disappears. Nicolas is aware of the danger that he poses. 'Stevens n'aurait jamais dû revenir parmi nous.' (31)

The return of Stevens coincides with the crisis in Nicolas's life when he is no longer able to endure the sterility and lack of physical attraction of his wife, Irene, and starts to look elsewhere for sexual satisfaction. He can see that he is succumbing to the violent, lustful side of his character which he shares with the other men of Griffin Creek, but he seems powerless to resist. He even tries to avoid his guilt. After Perceval has seen him fondling Nora in the boathouse, he accuses her of bringing sin into Griffin Creek. He has already used violence on her when he slapped her face for flirting with the American visitor. In the boathouse he only just restrains himself from attacking her savagely. As Bishop has argued, this is another example of the truly guilty party shifting the blame onto the victim in an effort to avoid the responsibility for the breach of social convention (1993, 176).

> Pensons aussi aux avances que fait le pasteur Nicolas Jones à sa nièce, Nora. Dans ce deuxième cas aussi, la transgression des valeurs sociales officielles, loin d'être punie par la société, aboutit au châtiment de ses victimes: sentiment de culpabilité chez Nora (qui ne sait repousser les injustes accusations du pasteur selon qui ce qui est arrivé était de sa faute à elle, et que c'est par elle que le péché est entré à Griffin Creek, FB 129; suicide d'Irène Jones, épouse du pasteur, en apprenant le comportement de son mari envers leur nièce, FB 129-30). Le texte hébertien fait siennes ici les affirmations féministes et autres selon lesquelles les victimes d'abus sexuel - le plus souvent femmes et enfants - sont doublement victimes, puisqu'elles tendent à s'en sentir coupables, sans doute en raison des valeurs qu'une société patriarcale leur a inculquées.

The real effect of the return of Stevens, however, is that after the events of 1936 the community collapses. All who can, move away, and Nicolas Jones is left at the head of an ever-dwindling community surrounded and outnumbered by the new village of francophone Catholics nearby. He is left with little to do except preach to an ever smaller number of parishioners, tyrannise over the twins and come to terms with his own guilt. Nicolas Jones is waiting for the Day of Judgement in the hope that finally God will be able to give him forgiveness and the peace of mind which he can never give himself.

The survenant himself, Stevens Brown, is also affected by his return to Griffin Creek. Indeed, Neil Bishop suggests that returning to Griffin Creek is the great error in Stevens's life, with dire consequences for the community (1993, 159).

> L'erreur de Stevens a peut-être été de revenir dans son pays, d'y prendre "racine dans le ventre d'une femme" (FB 69), (même s'il déclare son intention de repartir bientôt de Griffin Creek), car métonymiquement Américain, il ramène des États-Unis le viol et le meurtre.

He is forced to look into his own personality, as is his uncle, Nicolas Jones, and accept the depths to which he could sink and to confront the violence in his own character. Sénécal argues that he is well aware of the cause of his violence (56).

> Stevens recognizes the instinct of the cold executioner present within him as the dark workings of incest.

When he returns to the village, he is a selfish, ruthless and amoral young man. He has worked his way back from Florida where he had shared a house with his friend, Old Mic, whose role is to serve as an audience for Stevens's thoughts and recollections. He has no intention of staying in the village. This is to be a brief visit to assert his independence before he quits it forever. Guillemette makes the point that Stevens is barely back in the village when he is planning business activities with old Mic and envisaging his future life in Florida to which he longs to take his siblings so that they can escape from the life they lead with their parents (345).

> A peine rentré donc, Stevens élabore des projets d'association commerciale avec son ami américain et envisage l'avenir sous le soleil floridien, vivant de la vente des oranges...l'odyssée signifie le rejet du pays natal dans la mesure où Stevens souhaiterait voir ses cadets échapper à des parents dangereux et se rendre dans une contrée éloignée de Griffin Creek.

Stevens sticks firmly to his plan, working for Maureen as her hired man, drinking and going to town with his cousins in search of prostitutes and flirting with Nora and Olivia to pass the time. Throughout his stay he is detached about the village and his relations. His misogyny is never far beneath the surface, and it is aggravated by the behaviour of the women in the village, especially Nora and Olivia, who tantalise him in very different ways. Guillemette sees him as a man highly desired by the women of the village and made all the more attractive by his links with the USA (351).

> ...l'on peut penser que le texte propose déjà, de par son coefficient étatsunien la dimension d'un Stevens Brown intensément convoité par les personnages féminins des *Fous de Bassan*.

The return to the village makes Stevens think about what he wants - to escape for ever from this cold, northern outpost which he associates with violence and persecution. For him Florida is the symbol of warmth, freedom and happiness. His plans are made, and his departure is announced. He has every intention of leaving on the first of September with the money he has earned at Maureen's to return to Florida.

Instead he gives way to the violence within him to carry out a brutal double murder on his defenceless cousins. He has already been excited by the violent three-day storm which paralleled the violence within him, and, throughout his narrative, he insists that a similar storm was raging on the night that he went down to the beach with Nora and Olivia. The wind and the waves were raging, the sea birds shrieking, and the noise that they created matched the fury that was pounding inside his head. The presence of the two girls, the violence of Nora's denunciation, her attack on his masculinity (so important to the men of Griffin Creek) combine to send Stevens temporarily out of control. His violence changes his life permanently. He is arrested, charged and lucky enough to have the case dismissed because of the police tactics. He never sees Florida or Old Mic again. Instead he fights in the Second World War where his career is marked by the same violence as his stay in Griffin Creek, and he emerges permanently damaged mentally, for, as Bishop argues, he is marked definitively by his war service which signals his exile and alienation from his community (1993, 159). He spends the rest of his life in hospital with the other war-wounded, cared for by nuns and deprived of sex except when the men are allowed down to the rue Sainte-Catherine where some of them are able to pick up the young tarts who patrol there. Finally Stevens escapes with his stolen drugs and waits for death in his rented room, turning night into day and day into night and passing the time by writing to Old Mic. His life too has been ruined by the events of the summer of 1936.

The return of Stevens marks the beginning of the end for Griffin Creek. To Sénécal he is the antichrist (156). Hitherto the community has been united, able to keep secret its sins and its cruelty. The disappearance of the Atkins cousins brings the police in force into the village. Although the community closes ranks, Stevens is arrested, and a confession is forced from him. Despite his acquittal because of the methods used by the police, he never returns to his birthplace, spending the rest of his life in exile in the army or the hospital. All the minor characters are affected. Stevens's parents, John and Bea Atkins, are finally able to get rid of their children whom they never wanted. The distress of Ben and Alice Atkins, the parents of Nora, is not described in detail, but Patrick and Sidney, Olivia's brothers, and their father are maddened with grief. They feel guilty that they have failed to protect Olivia and furious about the attack on their property. The suffering of the village during the police investigation is described through the words of Perceval and *autres voix* which bring out the helplessness and the dismay of the people faced with this crime. From that time on, the community disintegrates. Nicolas Jones realises that they no longer wished to know each other. Bishop argues that the return of Stevens exposes the hypocrisy of the village which, while subscribing to conventional morality, is actually riddled with male chauvinism. The acceptance of this hypocrisy by society as a whole is symbolised by Stevens's acquittal, so that his perpetration of the ultimate crimes of murder and rape goes unpunished, as Bishop points out (1993, 175).

> Comportement que ce roman présente comme immoral, voire marginal par rapport aux valeurs que la société *prétend* défendre, mais en conformité secrète avec les valeurs sexistes réelles d'une société patriarcale et machiste comme le prouverait l'observation par laquelle se termine le roman: Stevens a été acquitté. *(FB 249)*

Through her use of the character of a survenant, Anne Hébert shows how an inbred and secretive community self-destructs after the return of one of its sons. Stevens is always potentially violent and has been emotionally damaged by the treatment of his parents. He blames his mother, in particular, for her cold, unloving nature, but his relatives can see that the cruel, violent streak is already present in his father who is seen as a dangerous man. As Sénécal says, his violence stems from his childhood (156). 'The destructive forces within Stevens' self are rooted deep within a childhood of violence.' No one escapes unscathed from the presence of Stevens, ruthlessly ready to take his revenge on his mother by making any woman who crosses his path suffer. Stevens is probably the most damaging and dangerous of all the survenants who figure in Québécois literature. He kills the innocent, exposes the inner secrets of the village and leaves behind a trail of violence and destruction. He is all the more dangerous, because, as Knight suggests, he seems to believe that he has power over himself and others (104).

> If Stevens Brown is caught in the illusion that he has the power to manipulate his own destiny, he is no less convinced he can also, at will, manœuvre the destiny of others.

The anglophone community of Griffin Creek will shortly disappear as the few, remaining inhabitants die off. Stevens is a survenant who leaves nothing but evil in his wake as he rouses the evil forces latent in the community and succumbs to the evil within himself. As such, Hébert's survenant is a completely new development in the genre. As Bishop says, Anne Hébert has used her novel to express her criticisms of the male-oriented society which can leave such crimes unpunished (1993, 224).

> ...Les Fous de Bassan se termine par l'expression...de la révolte de l'auteure contre un système politico-juridico-policier qui laisse impunis le viol et le meurtre...

Such social criticism, coupled with the feminist subtext and the violence of the climax, distinguishes the work of Anne Hébert from the other novels considered so far and paves the way for a novel of the nineties which will take up the themes of social violence and social criticism, but instead of the feminism, which is so important in the work of Anne Hébert, introduces the theme of interracial conflict.

Cowboy; Louis Hamelin

One of the authors to whom Louis Hamelin acknowledges a debt is Germaine Guèvremont, as he said in his interview with Jean Royer in 1991 (D-1): 'Je connaissais quelques classiques comme *Le Survenant* de Germaine Guèvremont.' The influence of *Le Survenant* can be seen in his partly autobiographical novel, *Cowboy*, seen by Mailhot as marking a distinct advance on his earlier works (217).

> *Cowboy* (1992), indépendamment de sa longueur, a beaucoup plus de poids, de chair, dans une Abitibi quasi magique à force de réalisme.

The book is called after a young native American, Cowboy, who becomes a friend of a young Montréalais, Gilles Deschênes. Gilles works for part of a year in the store in Grande-Ourse, a remote village in northern Quebec, and the novel begins soon after his arrival and finishes after his return to Montreal. Hamelin passed some time working in a store in the north where he encountered at first hand the tensions between the Whites and Indians of the region, as he explained in an interview with Marie-Claude Fortin (12-13).

> Louis Hamelin s'en allait, entre deux sessions d'études en création littéraire, travailler dans le magasin général d'une pourvoirie. Dans un village de quatre-vingts habitants, coupé du monde, séparé d'une réserve indienne par la voie ferrée. "J'ai passé quatre mois dans ce village, raconte Hamelin. J'ai travaillé, j'ai rencontré des Indiens, je suis allé sur la réserve, pendant un pow-wow. L'une des choses qui m'a le plus frappé, dès les premiers jours où j'ai mis les pieds là, c'est l'animosité, ancestrale, entre les Indiens et les Blancs. Et la virulence du discours des Blancs. Le racisme, les préjugés profondément ancrés, entretenus et transmis, et la profonde opposition de nature et de caractère."

He has recognised in an interview with Lucie Côté, which took place at almost the same time as the interview with Marie-Claude Fortin, that in *Cowboy* he made use of these experiences (B-1,4).

> L'histoire du livre, qui est un peu l'histoire de l'auteur, avoue-t-il, veut transmettre une dérive, une espèce de déchirement entre deux mondes.

Thus the background of commercial activity in difficult circumstances and the sense of living in a community where violence is accepted and frequent, where racial tension is ever present, and few inhabitants of whatever colour have much to look forward to are based on fact, even if transmitted through the novelist's eye and voice. Hamelin points out in the interview with Fortin that he always works from the real to the fictional (12). 'Je travaille toujours à partir d'événements vecus que je transpose dans un cadre fictif.'

Unlike Guèvremont who adopts the position of ominiscient narrator, Hamelin makes his survenant the narrator for most of the text. The first person narrative describes the summer's events with a certain cynical detachment, as Gilles is perfectly aware that he is not committed to this community for more than one summer. He feels himself to be an outsider for various reasons. He is city-bred, university-educated and aware that he is only a temporary resident. His white skin makes him alien to the Kawiches. His youth separates him from most of the Whites. Why he is in Grande-Ourse is never explained in detail, which is typical of his self-centred and unrevealing attitude, as Allard notes (1992, D-3). 'Son narrateur, dont on ne sait pratiquement rien des origines sinon qu'il a fait des études...' His arrival is not described, and his departure takes place without comment and abruptly so that at one moment he is still in the north, at the next he is back in Montreal reporting on events since his departure. He is a narrator who allows the reader to make his or her own deductions about the effect of his presence on the people who made up the remote community, as he is aware from the beginning that he is an intruder. 'Parachuté là comme commis je me cantonnais dans mes quartiers...' (14). The first-person narrative is interspersed with sections of prose written in a different register and marked off from Gilles's narrative both by format (they are inset) and typeface (italics) which Allard interprets as reflecting the thoughtfulness typical of Hamelin's work (1992, D-3). 'La mise en parallèle des deux narrations témoignent de la réflexion qui préside à l'écriture, ici comme dans les autres romans d'Hamelin.' These interruptions in the narrative refer to the tragic events of some twelve years before when a young Kawiche, Roméo Flamand, was gunned down outside the hotel of Jacques Boisvert. Roméo had been at the centre of a disturbance earlier but, at the moment of his murder, was peacefully leaving the scene with a bottle of beer given to him by Gilles Boisvert, the weakling son of Jacques. The flashbacks are, in fact, narrated in the voice of Gilles Boisvert and represent his tormented thoughts as he tries to make sense of the events of so many years ago, to determine whether it was really he who fired the shot and committed the murder for which he went to prison, or whether it was his father, who was beside him at the time. The interplay of the two narratives, neither complete in itself, enables the reader bit by bit to piece together the events of long ago as perceived by Gilles Deschênes and to understand their effect on the atmosphere in Grande-Ourse. Gilles Boisvert, for his part, ultimately comes to understand that he shares the guilt for the murder of Roméo with his father, who fired first.

>...Gilles le regarde partir et la carabine entre ses mains, mais ne fera rien parce que jamais parce que tu ne tueras point mais à sa droite soudain le voilà qui est là Jacques Boisvert en personne son père une apparition il est revenu sans bruit de ses dévotions lubriques auprès de cette bonne femme de la haute qui s'est laissée tringler sur quelque îlot désert avec de la mousse pour tout confort pendant que le mari en fauteuil roulant les roues bloquées sur le quai, oh Boisvert est là, maintenant, on dirait qu'il sait tout, qu'il a tout vu tout entendu, tout analysé saisi assimilé en un éclair photographique et il épaule cette puissante carabine, cette carabine au téléscope ominiscient ce gros calibre dont le canon sexué devient progressivement parallèle à la terre et Gilles, cette fois, cette fois, Gilles, Vroum un premier coup troue la nuit, quand vous vous tenez juste à côté ça veut vous jeter à terre un tel coup de feu, Broum le père qui tire et donne l'exemple l'exemplaire père Gilles épaule lui aussi l'impulsion c'est contagieux cette position et le tonnerre se propage la violence viscérale Vroum Gilles a tiré à son tour ça devient un duo dans le dos de l'Indien qui a disparu Broum on tire quand même dans la direction approximative on tire dans le noir on tire comme pour tuer toute la nuit tout ce qu'elle cache protège exacerbe depuis toujours la fusillade retentit dans tout le village tous ils l'entendent Boisvert a tiré le premier Gilles a tiré ensuite... (404-405)

In this way Hamelin enables the reader to enjoy a privileged position by giving access to the two accounts, whereas Gilles Deschênes, the newcomer, has to depend on what the villagers and the Kawiches tell him, which is little, for his understanding of preceding events. As for Gilles Boisvert, one of the actors in the drama that happened years ago, he is in exile not daring to return to the village.

It is the beginning of summer when the novel opens, and Gilles Deschênes has recently started work in the village store where Benoît, the manager, and le Vieux try to explain to him the sort of community in which he will be working. Right from the start he is made aware that he is in a community with its own way of life and code of conduct. The rules of the city no longer apply. According to Le Vieux the Kawiches are not to be trusted. The north of Quebec is like the Wild West.

> La semaine précédant mon arrivée, le grand Alexandre et sa bande, petites frappes notoires et fauteurs de troubles familiers des centres de redressement de la région avait fait régner la loi du Far West à Grande-Ourse. (29)

The Whites are surrounded by the Kawiches who, in the opinion of Le Vieux, are not far removed from a state of savagery and of whom he has the most unfavorable opinions. '- Sans nous autres, ils auraient encore des peaux de bêtes au cul'(65). Gilles quickly discovers that most of the other Whites in the village share this attitude. Brawls between Whites and Kawiches are a regular feature of local life, although Jacques Boisvert, when he is present, by sheer force of personality and physical force if necessary, can usually keep some sort of order. Gilles does not fit easily into this society and quickly becomes an irritant. He is not attracted by the local Whites. He finds them suspicious, malevolent and uninteresting. He does not share their attitude to the Kawiches and is indifferent to their disapproval of his growing friendship with some of the younger members of the tribe. From the first appearance of Cowboy and his friends Gilles is drawn towards them, which was the experience of Hamelin himself, as Fortin states (12). 'Hamelin se sentait attiré par la délinquance des jeunes Indiens de la réserve.' He ignores the warnings of Benoît and is not unduly concerned about following the rules in refusing credit to the Indians, who soon discover the weak points of the storekeepers.

> Benoît semblait craindre, de ma part, une bienveillance excessive à l'égard de la gent autochtone. Il prenait maintenant soin d'émailler son discours de fines allusions à la présence de ces fainéants à nos portes et il me suggérait à mots couverts de faire le ménage dans mes amitiés. (121)

The Kawiches exploit these weaknesses skilfully to get as much as they can on credit, as they have usually already spent their social security in the bars of the towns further south where they had to go to get their social security benefits. Gilles is quickly identified as a possible weak link in the store, as he himself readily admits.

> En surface, je restais le gentil gérant. En surface, je faisais respecter l'injonction des actionnaires et les apparences étaient sauves; tout crédit avait été coupé aux Indiens. Le soir, après onze heures, je consentais à des arrangments. (336)

His lack of moral scruples and his sympathy for the Kawiches mean that he shows little concern for his responsibilities as an employee of the Pourvoirie whose financial problems are aggravated. His weakness towards the Kawiches also worsens their financial position, which Gilles knows. He is too much their ally to resist their demands, however, and his weakness is known and resented by the other Whites, another destabilising element in the village. He is perfectly aware of his attitude towards the Kawiches.

> -T'es mon ami, Gilles? demanda Cowboy.
> Je répondis que oui, même si ce Cowboy restait à mes yeux l'inconnu incarné. Car il ne m'attirait pas tant comme individu que comme exemplaire, produit de sa culture. Notre amitié n'avait de sens qu'au pluriel. C'était une amitié de fond, indifférente aux détails dont se composent habituellement les affinités. C'est l'Indien que j'aimais en Cowboy. Je me rendais parfaitement compte de cette discrimination positive. (39)

His fondness for socialising with the Kawiches is another factor in his alienation from the local Whites. He spends evenings drinking with the young Kawiches and soon becomes one of the lovers of Judith, a beautiful single mother, abandoned by the white father of her child not long before the wedding he had promised (215). Judith and the young men all use naphtha to help them escape from the sordid reality of their lives, but Gilles, although more than happy to drink with them, will not join in the drug sniffing. He is warned by Cowboy and his friends that his affair with Judith may cause trouble, as she is the girl friend of a very dangerous member of the tribe, currently in prison, but soon to be released, le grand Alexandre. Gilles is not particularly impressed at the time but later has cause to remember the warning, when he discovers the extent of Alexandre's resentment. Too drunk to care and with a willing girl at his disposal, he is insouciant about the future. His activities are thus as potentially disruptive to relations between the Kawiches as to relations between the Whites and the Kawiches.

The other Whites can just about tolerate his fondness for the company of the Kawiches as long as he consorts with them out of doors, but, when he goes to the hotel with the Kawiches to drink in the bar, he quickly discovers that his behaviour has been noticed and is very much resented.

> Je sentais peser sur moi les charges d'une accusation inexprimée. J'étais en train de commettre une nette entorse à la règle, à la loi orale du pays. Qui étais-je donc, misérable employé des possesseurs honnis, pour choisir ainsi mes potes? (151)

The white men are aggressively hostile to this outsider who is breaking their code and is seen as a traitor to his race and social group. He is despised as the employee of a company whose activities are resented in the locality. The men are all the more resentful in that in the past they have made gestures of friendship towards him.

> Le trappeur déclara, après m'avoir coiffé de sa barbe;
> - Votre problème, à la Pourvoirie, c'est les Boucanés! Si tu commences à frayer avec eux autres, t'as pas fini, mon commis...
> - Les Boucanés?
> - Ben oui, les Kawiches...Les Indiens! traduisit Legris.
> Je remerciai l'homme de cet avertissement désintéressé. (145)

They had warned him to beware of the Kawiches as had le Vieux. They had expected him to conform. His failure to do so means that they become angry when they see him joining with men they despise and, in a very real sense, fear. As Le Vieux has pointed out to Gilles, the fertility of Kawiche women is such that they all have enormous families of pure blood or métis children, and as a result the Whites seem to fear that the territory will revert to the Indians. '*Ça va revirer territoire indien...*' (346) Judith's child is a métis, and Gilles is well aware that many of the Indian women are ready to prostitute themselves to railway employees in return for free travel, but the consequence is very often a half-caste child, whose white father makes every possible effort to avoid accepting responsibility. Gilles can see the hypocrisy of this attitude, which does nothing to make him feel more sympathetic towards the Whites.

Gilles's own sexual life is quite complicated as he is also sleeping with Brigitte, the mistress of Jacques Boisvert, who runs the hotel for Boisvert and gets bored during his frequent absences when he is inspecting his property further north. For Brigitte, Gilles is a new and reasonably attractive face, who reminds her of the Montreal which she left to come and live with Boisvert. Their couplings are energetic and often bizarre as when he makes love to her over the store's freezer, only to be caught *in flagrante* by Boisvert himself, whose reaction is remarkably restrained in the circumstances. He pushes Brigitte into the ice and ignores Gilles who had no idea what to expect. Boisvert does not, in the event, seem to bear any particular ill-will towards either of the lovers. Brigitte, however, does resent Gilles's affair with Judith, although she seems to accept that it is inevitable that a man will sleep with a Kawiche girl if he gets the chance. Gilles has to endure some barbed remarks, but overall his complicated love life does not cause him nearly as many problems as might be expected. What does alarm him is the undisguised lubricity of many of the Kawiche women, even those who are considerably older than he is, who grope him without hesitation when they get the chance and make it quite clear that they would be prepared to go much further if he were in the slightest interested.

> Grand-mère Fernande, adipeuse et bonasse, enfoncée dans la camionnette, me déshabilla d'un regard charmant, abruti, et m'obligea à reculer de quelques pas lorsque, après avoir jeté au loin sa bouteille vide, sa main parcheminée montra un intérêt marqué pour mes parties. (248)

Their rapaciousness can even shock their own families who do not enjoy the sight of an older Kawiche woman trying to seduce a young white man. Again the presence of Gilles can unintentionally cause disputes within the community, in this case between the Kawiche women.

The presence of the newcomer therefore causes disruption in the community almost from the beginning. His marked preference for the company of the Kawiches alienates and infuriates the Whites. Although he can see quite clearly that his policy of allowing the Kawiches to extend their credit and thus put themselves further into debt is not in their interest, he is constrained by his feelings of friendship for them. While the Kawiches think that they are exploiting the store and cheating it, in a very real sense they are the ones who are being exploited, as they will never be out of debt. They can never escape from the power of the store. César Flamand, the father of the murdered Roméo, is a prime example. He is engaged by the company to decorate the holiday chalets which are also part of its business, but all his wages are already committed to paying off his debts even before he has earned them. Gilles resents this on behalf of his friends and is none too careful about keeping accurate accounts, which further worsens the financial position of the store and eventually threatens the jobs of those who work there. This does not greatly concern Gilles for whom the work in Grande-Ourse is only a stopgap anyway. His careless attitude has serious consequences for both Le Vieux and Benoît whose jobs are threatened as the store's financial position deteriorates, and they suffer from the strain of the financial worry and the increased presence of the Kawiches, attracted by their friendship with Gilles. Ultimately both men fall ill.

Gilles's affair with Judith is potentially extremely disruptive, should Alexandre get to hear of it. His affair with Brigitte adds an element of tension to the life of the village, although it too does not seem to have any immediate repercussions. Nonetheless Gilles's arrival has introduced a new and disturbing element into the village, which has never forgotten the events of twelve years earlier. Gilles is mildly curious about his namesake and about the death of Roméo which is the element which continually poisons the relations between the Whites and the Kawiches. He realises that before his arrival the two sides had coexisted in a spirit of mutual detestation by largely ignoring each other. Even after the brawls in the bar at night both sides would resume the same policy of apparent indifference the next morning.

> Les deux petits mondes pouvaient coexister avec leurs lois propres, parallèles, en l'absence de tout contact apparent. On se flairait et on se montrait les dents, on s'abouchait en aveugles dans la nuit, c'était un accident. Le jour suivant, on recommençait à s'ignorer, à haïr cet ailleurs proche. Quelques dizaines de pieds, c'était l'abîme. Un seul point commun subsistait, écrasant toutes les différences; l'indifférence des uns, l'indifférence des autres. (148)

This state of affairs has lasted for the twelve years after the murder for which Gilles Boisvert was sentenced. The Kawiches had sullenly accepted the verdict although without exception they believed that the actual killer was Jacques Boisvert, which, as the flashbacks of his son indicate, was almost certainly the case. During these years they gave little overt sign of the resentment for which they had so many causes, but the local Whites are not fooled. Le Vieux warns Gilles.

> - J'ai entendu de quoi vous parliez...Les Indiens oublient jamais une affaire comme ça.
> - Quelle affaire?
> Il clappa de la langue et poursuivit:
> - L'affaire de l'hôtel! Si le jeune Boisvert revient ici, c'est un homme mort! Fini! Il remettra jamais les pieds à Grande- Ourse! Il est barré à vie! (67)

Jacques Boisvert, who is the only White in the area to take an interest in the Kawiches even though they regard him as their enemy, explains to Gilles that the government had forcibly moved the Kawiches to a new reserve as the old one was needed for a reservoir and was flooded as part of the hydro-electric schemes of northern Quebec. The reserve to which the Kawiches were sent turned out to be infested with mosquitoes and disease so that in the end the Indians had to move again. The new reserve is surrounded by the reservoir on three sides and on the fourth by the taiga, so that it is extremely remote. When Gilles visits it at the invitation of Cowboy, he realises that he is one of a handful of white faces, and far from help should he need it. Apart from the problem inherent in the reservation system, the ancestral lands of the Kawiches have been ruined by the Pourvoirie, the company which owns the store where Gilles works. It has conducted extensive logging activities in the area, with the result that the roads are lined with a thin screen of trees behind which is the desolation left by the loggers. The activities of the hydro-electric engineers have left their mark also, so that the countryside is polluted with debris and litter to which the Kawiches add considerably as they jettison thoughtlessly the waste products of modern civilisation like the plastic which wraps the convenience foods which they adore. Gilles realises that even Boisvert contributes to the alienation and dispossession of the Kawiches, as he employs young Kawiches to build holiday chalets on the remote lakes, pays them a decent wage and forbids them any alcohol, so that by the end of the season they will have some money to their name. Nonetheless the longer-term effect will be that another lake will be surrounded by the holiday homes reserved for the Whites from the south, and the Kawiches will no longer frequent an area that once had been theirs. The treatment of their women, the loss of their ancestral lands, the loss of their way of life and, in a very real sense, their raison d'être all fuel the resentment of the Kawiches. They despise the Whites, particularly the Americans who do not understand their way of life or the country into which they are penetrating, as Paola Ruggeri points out (23).

> En généralisant, on pourrait dire que l'Amérindien demeure impénétrable pour le Québécois, malgré les affinités existant entre eux, telle que l'aversion mal cachée pour la culture états-unienne.

The most striking example of the latter is the reaction of the Kawiches when American bear-hunters kill a female bear with three cubs out of season, procured for them by Jacques Boisvert so that they will not go home empty-handed with their holiday ruined to spread hostile propaganda about the area as a base for hunters and tourists. They indicate contemptuously to Gilles that all the cubs will die as a result of this fawning effort to conciliate the disappointed Americans.

- Les Américains, dit Cowboy, ils ont tué leur ours.
Il plissait les paupières, comme extrêmement sceptique sous cette lumière assommante.
- Ouais. Avec l'aide de Boisvert...Boisvert, sa mélasse et sa couenne de lard.
- Boisvert.
- Une mère ourse avec trois petits, nota le Kid en regardant le sol.
- Trois? Vous êtes sûrs?
- Trois, répondit Cowboy.
- Qu'est-ce qu'ils vont faire, sans leur mère?
Des hochements songeurs agitaient les têtes.
- Mourir, dit Cowboy. (295-96)

Yet the Americans are far more sensitive to the landscape and will pick up their litter. The gulf of incomprehension between the two sides is almost unbridgeable as Gilles discovers when forced to act as an interpreter for the Americans. On more than one occasion Gilles is witness to the intensity of the mutual loathing of the two sides.

The arrival of Gilles Deschênes introduces a disturbing element into this mix of tacit hatred and resentment on both sides. His refusal to side with the other Whites, who expect him to be one of them, attracts their enmity towards not only him but the Kawiches as well. The Kawiches are ready to fight. The Indian-White hostility is inbred in them from schoodays as Gilles Boisvert remembers, when there was racial warfare in the playground with rocks flying from either side.

La cour de récré. Les guerres de races. Les roches qui volaient d'un côté et de l'autre. Indiens en bande contre les Blancs. (147)

Aware of the sympathy that Gilles feels for them, the Kawiches become slightly bolder in opposing the Whites. Relations are further worsened through no fault of Gilles, when the most promising of the young Indians, Admiral Nelson, is drowned in a flood of beer from an overturned lorry which he is helping to lift upright. Gilles does feel slightly guilty that he had not reacted more quickly to the warning signs that the lorry was about to topple over, but there was little he could have done to save the young man. The Kawiches do not blame him, as it is Le Vieux whose incompetence is the real cause of the disaster. Le Vieux had put the lorry into the ditch as Jacques Boisvert does not hesitate to point out, although Le Vieux instantly gets his revenge by recalling the events of twelve years ago, which silences Boisvert.

Son doigt haineux dessinait la suite dans l'air lourd devant lui.
-Toi, Boisvert!...trouva-t-il encore la force de haleter. Couper les ponts! Douze ans! Le sang! Onze coups! Mes doigts dans les trous! La vérité, Boisvert, la vérité, hein?
Il délirait quasiment.
L'autre ne répondit pas mais il restait là, il avait blêmi. (163)

During the furious exchanges between the two men the lorry is almost forgotten, so that, when it suddenly topples over with Nelson still waiting patiently beside it to help, almost everyone had forgotten about him. Gilles cannot immediately remember why he is worried, and it is Le Vieux who suddenly realises the full extent of the tragedy.

Gilles is the witness of these events rather than the instigator, but his growing friendship with the Kawiches leads to an invitation from Cowboy to come to the reserve for the summer pow-wow when the Kawiches turn once again to their traditional sports, and the party lasts for at least a week. Boisvert has already warned him to be careful, as in the end he will find himself a White alone amongst a hundred enemies and that when that happens, he will have no one to thank but himself.

- Attention à tes fréquentations, Gilles. Tu changeras jamais la couleur de ta peau. Quand ils seront à cent contre toi, je te souhaite bonne chance. (354)

Gilles does not take the warning too seriously. His summer has been a hedonistic one with plenty of sex and drink, while his work did not get in the way of his enjoyment. Only occasionally does he feel seriously involved as when he protects Salomé, a beautiful, Kawiche teenager from the drunken assault of her grandfather who with his second wife is fostering her. Gilles could have her for the asking, but restrains himself even when presented with the opportunity. The death of Nelson has shocked him, especially when he realises the callousness with which it was viewed by the other Whites. Only Boisvert seems to care. A four-wheel drive full of American tourists come to hunt bear arrives on the scene just after the realisation of the tragedy, and immediately Le Vieux starts to fuss over them, ignoring his upturned lorry. With a staggering lack of sensitivity the Americans start to film everything, as if the tragedy has been staged for their benefit, and are only persuaded to desist when the corpse is about to be brought to the surface thanks entirely to the efforts of Boisvert.

A far worse shock for Gilles, however, is the death of Cowboy. Cowboy is a superb swimmer who has already frightened Gilles by the length of time he can stay under water, but he has confessed to Gilles during one of their drunken sessions in a moment of masculine intimacy that, when he is in the water, he can feel the spirit of Nelson trying to retain him. He has no wish to live to be old. '...ne voulait pas vivre vieux' (177). Gilles is not convinced, although he is aware that the Kawiches for the most part no longer feel that there is any reason to continue to live. Only Nelson had a goal in life.

> L'Amiral Nelson était un solitaire, déjà accoutumé de ne pouvoir compter dans le monde que sur un minimum de compassion. C'était un jeune Amérindien d'une dizaine d'années, enjoué comme le diable mais capable d'humeur sérieuse...A la différence d'une majorité de frères, sœurs, cousins et cousines, Nelson faisait des plans d'avenir et, chaque hiver, sur les collines couvertes de pins gris, il trappait la martre pour avoir les moyens de ses rêves. Il voulait devenir ingénieur, passer son brevet de pilote et s'acheter un hydravion. (54)

Yet he is dead through no fault of his own. Cowboy's suicide is therefore no great surprise to the alert reader, but Gilles is devastated by the loss of his friend, for friend is what Cowboy had become. They had even got over their mutual jealousy over Salomé to whom both were attracted and confided their most intimate secrets to each other.

> Cowboy répétait sans arrêt, sur le même ton pointu;
> - T'es mon ami, hein, Gilles? T'es mon ami, hein?
> - On est les plus grands amis de la terre, Cowboy.
> - Je suis ton ami, Gilles.
> - Oui. Oui.
> Nous nous promîmes alors toutes sortes de choses. Je l'encourageai à flirter avec Brigitte qui le trouvait pas mal du tout, si si, elle me l'avait dit, il m'implora de recoucher avec Judith, il arrangerait la chose pour moi, oui oui, ce serait facile, je lui parlai de Salomé, de cet amour tendre et sacré véritable dilection qui me rappelait les affres de mon enfance sauf que cette fois, il avait la redoutable impasse du sexe, et il m'assura que rendu au fond des choses, l'amour était partout pareil et pour se décharger de ses humeurs, à tout prendre, il préférait les vraies grosses comme Gisèle dont il me vanta le coup de reins en des termes évasifs et choisis, et ce lac volcanique qu'elle avait entre les jambes. (362)

Gilles determines that he must go to the reservation for Cowboy's funeral and then be present at the pow-wow. He completely fails to anticipate what awaits him.

> A part le gérant du magasin de la Baie d'Hudson les faces blêmes comme la mienne pouvaient se compter sur les doigts d'une seule main dans le secteur. (381)

Cowboy's family welcomes him, but none of them feels the same degree of responsibility for him as Cowboy, although Christophe, Cowboy's brother, warns Gilles that many of the tribe are to be avoided and that there are parts of the reservation to which he should never go alone. '- Viens jamais ici tout seul! me conseilla-t-il sèchement.' (374) Gilles is soon aware of the brooding hostility of Alexandre, the lover of Judith, and realises that the sporting activities of the pow-wow are only an excuse for a debauch on a massive scale. He is deeply moved by the funeral conducted in Algonquin by one of the tribal elders, although he understands nothing of what is said and cannot communicate directly with the elder who has no French.

> Des cantiques lancinants, tirés de missels catholiques traduits en algonquin, montaient dans l'air moite et redescendaient doucement, bientôt repris en choeur par l'assemblée. La voix plaintive de l'ancêtre me parut si poignante à travers ma fatigue qu'un étau enserra aussitôt ma gorge. Elle s'éraillait savamment, s'enflait et se déployait en spires hypnotiques et en serpentements berceurs avant de retomber, de s'étrangler et de s'effilocher, simple lien serré et cassant entre les coeurs, flottant dans l'air comme une main immatérielle. (374)

After the funeral he gets sucked into the revelry. The Kawiches are convinced that he has come for no other reason than to sleep with as many Indian girls as possible, although he does manage to convince some of them that he came for the sake of Cowboy. Even then they will only accept that he came for Cowboy and to sleep with the girls.

> Tous les Indiens avec qui je liais conversation se disaient persuadés que je me trouvais là pour les filles. J'avais beau leur parler de Cowboy, de la mort de Cowboy, ils ne se résignaient qu'à moitié et s'accrochaient à un compromis; j'avais couvert toute cette distance pour dire adieu à mon ami **et** pour rencontrer un tas de filles. (384)

Kawiche sexual morality is not that of the Whites, but Gilles quickly realises that under White influence the old traditions have been debauched. The Kawiche girls will sleep with anyone, White or

Indian, and their men simultaneously take advantage of that and resent it when Whites also take advantage of it. Gilles loses all respect on the reservation when he allows himself to be seduced by a notorious man-eater. Too drunk to resist, he allows her to pull him into her hut, despite the warnings of Christophe that he will probably contract Aids from her. The following morning Gilles has lost his self-respect.

> Je sortis de cette catastrophe avec l'âme en pièces détachées... Il ne me restait plus qu'à me demander ce que je faisais là, moi avec mes pensées stériles et mon désespoir comme un poignard. (385)

Too alarmed about his chances of leaving the reservation safely to care, he realises that he is now an object of hatred and contempt for many of the Kawiches. His behaviour has shocked them, and he is, in their eyes, no better than any other White. The Kawiche policeman on the reservation has no wish to get involved when Gilles finds himself threatened, and Gilles is left to seek a way of escape as best he can. César Flamand, who had brought him to the reservation, had promised to take him away when he was ready, but César, shattered by the death of Cowboy, is not only incapable of taking the boat across the reservoir, but, having started to drink again, is utterly confused. He thinks that Gilles is a Boisvert, the murderer of his son, and urges the other Indians to attack, as here at last is a chance for revenge. Gilles is saved only by the sudden appearance of Boisvert's aeroplane which unexpectedly roars across the reservation, to the consternation of the Kawiches. Further tragedy ensues when the plane crashes into the reservoir, resulting in the deaths of Boisvert and his passenger. The pow-wow which was on the point of being disrupted by the murder of one White is brought to an abrupt end by the accidental death of another, ironically a death for which the Kawiches had long been wishing.

With the death of Boisvert the hatred of the Kawiches seems appeased. Gilles succeeds in leaving the reservation and returns to Montreal where he still sees Brigitte, now pregnant with Boisvert's baby (unless, of course, Gilles is the father, which is a possibility, as he realises). From time to time he hears from Salomé about Grande-Ourse which the Kawiches have more or less abandoned. Very few of them ever visit it, and most of them have moved further north. Ruggeri points out that for the Amerindians Grande-Ourse has become an accursed place, and their withdrawal to the north is an

example of a new period of colonisation by the Québécois, which
may end in the total dispossession of the Indians (27).

> ...les Autochtones considèrent Grande-Ourse un lieu maudit, et qu'ils ont
> commencé à le déserter pour se diriger plus au nord. Voilà la signification
> première de la nordicité dans le roman: la néo-colonisation du territoire de
> la part des Québécois entraîne la disparition des Amérindiens, destinés à
> migrer jusqu'à ce qu'il n'y ait plus de nord pour eux.

Relations between the Whites and the Indians are worse than ever,
with very little contact at all.

> Salomé m'apprend qu'il y a presque plus d'Indiens dans ce coin. Les
> relations entre les deux communautés ne s'amélioraient guère et certains
> sont remontés vers le Nord. Plus personne ne campe aux portes du village.
> (416)

There are rare exceptions like Judith who has moved in with the
owner of the village restaurant who is about to divorce his wife,
presumably to marry Judith, while Christophe is hoping to study to
become a lawyer. Already the contacts with Grande-Ourse are
becoming fewer and further between. For Gilles it is clear that the
summer in the north is fading into a colourful episode of his past to
which he can look back with mingled feelings. Grande-Ourse,
however, will never be the same. The racial divide has deepened.
Both Whites and Kawiches have tragic memories to live with as four
people are dead. There has been no reconciliation, and the condition
of the Kawiches has deteriorated further.

Gilles is not directly responsible for much of this. He was in no way
responsible for the death of Nelson whom he had warned earlier of
the danger. He did not cause the suicide of Cowboy nor the deaths of
Boisvert and his passenger, but his presence probably hastened both.
Cowboy found in Gilles someone in whom he could confide. To
Gilles he voiced his thoughts about the future, his preference to die
young, his awareness of the call of the spirits of his people. It is
possible that his suicide is hastened by his awareness of his thoughts,
once he had voiced them to Gilles. Boisvert died on his way to the
reservation, a place he had no reason to visit unless he was on his way
to rescue Gilles, although Ruggeri makes the interesting suggestion
that Boisvert crashed his plane deliberately, a parallel to the suicide
of Cowboy (26, note 17). He knew that Gilles was going up there and
more than anyone else he was aware of the risks that Gilles was

running. The telephone call to the store, which Gilles made to try to summon help, seemed to bear no result, but Boisvert could have heard about it and be coming to his aid, when he crashed fatally.

Gilles's role is certainly destructive in other ways. He causes dissension in both communities by his sexual activities, and it is only thanks to the maturity and indifference of Boisvert that the outcome is not more serious for him. His sleeping around amongst the Kawiches very nearly results in his death and certainly causes great friction within some of the families affected. His behaviour in the store brings the looming financial crisis to a head, and he is seen, with some cause, to be behaving irresponsibly, if not dishonestly. By the end of the book Benoît has had to go south to recover from a near-breakdown, Le Vieux is a broken man and Lili, an ambitious and unscrupulous Kawiche, is installed in the store to run it with a rod of iron after the total failure of the men.

The most serious consequence of Gilles's summer has to be the deepening of the gulf between the two communities. When he arrives, they are able to coexist, however much they detest each other, and this is shown by their behaviour when both communities find themselves in the same place at the same time, for example at the station when the train arrives.

> A ces moments-là, le clivage était net et remarquable entre le village des Blancs et celui des Indiens. Les deux groupes, non miscibles, se côtoyaient sans contact, sans prendre acte l'un de l'autre. Le contrat social, dans ce coin-là, ne prévoyait rien de ce genre. (249)

After he leaves, they have as little contact as possible, as neither side wishes to understand or be involved with the other. Gilles's thoughtlessness and selfishness are partly responsible for this. He does not think about the consequences of his actions. Usually he is careless about the feelings of others. He amuses himself and seeks his pleasure where he can. Coming from a city environment, he does not appreciate the depth of racial feeling still existing in parts of the province and does not care if he inflames it by his lack of tact and sensitivity, as he is impatient where the attitudes of the other Whites are concerned.

He fills some of the role of Guèvremont's Survenant in that he comes to a community with a reasonably settled way of life, stays for a short period and leaves, but behind him everything has changed. The principal difference is that in Guèvremont the Survenant opened the eyes of some of the characters to the narrowness of their way of life. He introduced some positive ideas (an awareness of the wider world) as well as some negative ones (introducing Joinville Provençal to drink), but Gilles Deschênes does nothing positive. Quite unintentionally he makes a difficult situation worse. He means no harm to anyone, but he is still at an age to be irresponsible and hedonistic. He does not look to the future, with the result that he is taken unawares by the effects of some of his actions. His indifference to the feelings and opinions of others is another destructive element.

Hamelin has created a Survenant figure, who, in keeping with the overall tone of his novel, is much more destructive than Guèvremont's and who leaves behind him a community irreparably damaged, partly, but only partly, through his irresponsibility and hedonism. Self-absorbed and self-centred, Gilles Deschênes watches the community slowly self-destructing while never appreciating the extent of his own contribution to the process. He himself seems to emerge from the summer unscathed. He was shocked by the death of Cowboy and badly frightened by what happened to him on the reservation but the effects do not seem to be lasting. He settles back into Montreal aware that Grande-Ourse and its people are becoming more and more distant. He is still interested in them, but with a detachment which will soon fade into indifference. By continuing the story, even if only briefly, after the departure of Gilles from Grande-Ourse Hamelin lets us see how his Survenant character reacts to the period under review. In this he differs from Guèvremont whose Survenant disappears from the narrative the moment he leaves the village. To some extent Hamelin ties up the loose ends of the summer. Modern communications mean that it is easy for Gilles to keep in occasional contact with the people amongst whom he had lived and in whom he still has some interest. He has not been deeply affected by the events of the summer, not even the death of Cowboy, unlike the people amongst whom he lived. Grande-Ourse is behind him, and he can go on his insouciant way, while the Kawiches and their neighbours live out the consequences of the violence and hatred stirred up by the disruptive presence and careless attitude of Gilles Deschênes, who has exactly the mixture of qualities and defects to which Germaine Guèvremont refers and which makes her Survenant such a dangerous intruder into the lives of the Beauchemin family (Lepage, 1992, 152-3).

Conclusion

All five of the novels surveyed in the preceding chapters are concerned with characters who are wanderers, a feature they share with many other characters in other literatures and other times. The Survenant, Alain Dubois, Hervé Jodoin, Stevens Brown and Gilles Deschênes never become part of the communities to which they are temporarily attached and, except for Alain Dubois, they have no real wish to. Three of them, the Survenant, Stevens Brown and Gilles Deschênes never had any intention of staying for any length of time. Jodoin's intentions are ambiguous. He had no particular desire to go to Saint-Joachin, but once there he had no plan to leave until he was forced to depart by the scandal which he had caused. Against all advice Alain Dubois returns to Macklin after his three-month period of mourning, determined to force himself onto a community which has already clearly rejected him. In spirit if not in the flesh, he remains an outsider, a sort of survenant.

The original Survenant of Germaine Guèvremont conforms perfectly to Lavoie's description (25). Despite all his talents and his charm, in the end the Survenant leaves behind nothing but memories. There is no tangible memorial to him, only the silent adoration of Angélina which will last until her death. The Survenant understands his own character; the restlessness, the inability to find long-term satisfaction, his lack of a desire to establish a permanent relationship with another human being and his need for the excitement of constantly experiencing something new. He runs away from responsibility and security, leaving behind him a community which has been forced to examine its deepest beliefs. Lavoie also makes the interesting point that the Survenant, unlike the *coureurs de bois*, seems to travel east, the direction in which lies Europe (21).

> L'Est est en quelque sorte la direction oubliée, la route sans retour qui mène aux vieux pays. Or, paradoxalement, cette direction orientale est la seule dont nous sommes sûrs que le Survenant l'ait suivie pour un ultime voyage.

Again she sees this as a sign of weakness (21): 'La route de l'Est, dans cette perspective représente la fuite, le retour aux origines, le refus de la vie.'

In the other four novels looked at in this study, the survenant-type characters correspond to at least some of Lavoie's descriptors. Alain

Dubois also heads east from Montreal to Macklin where he fails utterly to inspire respect in the community or to lay a sure foundation for his marriage. Hervé Jodoin also probably heads east from Montreal to Saint-Joachin, where he casts a cynical and scornful eye on the petty hypocrisy and infighting of a small, provincial town. Stevens Brown goes even further east down the Saint Lawrence, and he alone returns to his birthplace. Once returned, he sets in motion all the tensions and cruelty of the inbred village community. Deeply flawed himself, Stevens wreaks far more havoc than any of the others. Unlike the others, he is not a complete outsider to the community, and he brings all his accumulated resentment and hatred back with catastrophic results. His misogynistic desire for revenge on the women of his village is satisfied by the brutal and callous double murder of his cousins, a murder of which he is never convicted. Gilles Deschênes heads north, unintentionally bringing sadness and tragedy to the Kawiches. Like Jodoin, but unlike Alain Dubois and Stevens Brown, he is relatively unaffected by the disasters that his presence helps to provoke and is able to return to Montreal to resume his life with only a few reminders of his summer in Grande-Ourse. All these characters share something of the flight from self-knowledge even when, like Jodoin, they claim to know their own motives perfectly. In different ways they all try to avoid responsibility for their actions and refuse to admit to their essential weakness and lack of self-control. In the hands of these five authors the theme of the survenant becomes the basis for a study of a flawed and divided society in which people struggle to come to terms with their inheritance and their role in the communities in which they live.

The universal theme of the 'stranger who comes to town' or the visitor has a particular importance in the literature of Quebec. Historical fact and cultural tradition have combined to create the image of the adventurer, whether he was called the *coureur de bois*, the *voyageur* or the *survenant*. All of them were free from many of the ties of society and in opposition to the *habitant* who stayed in his community to practise his trade or cultivate the land. All of them belong to the period when Quebec was predominantly a rural society, whose end can be seen approaching in *Le Survenant* with the arrival of motor cars in the village. The twentieth century saw the increasing urbanisation of Quebec, as Montreal, in particular, sucked in the surplus rural population as chronicled by Gabrielle Roy in *Bonheur d'occasion*. Quebec writers, however, did not abandon the theme of the survenant but instead adapted it to the changing conditions.

Whereas Guèvremont was writing about a remote, rural community into which came a stranger with a wide experience of eastern Canada, her successors turned to the conflict between the metropolis and the small, provincial towns (Langevin and Bessette), between the exile who returns from the USA to his native village and those who have stayed at home (Hébert), to the clash between the indigenous peoples of Northern Canada and their White conquerors (Hamelin). Whether the conflict is internalised, as in the case of Alain Dubois, or externalised as between the Kawiches and the local Whites, the theme is inextricably linked to conflict. Through conflict the characters are forced either to confront their flaws and weaknesses or to try to shun the reality of what they are and what they have done. Communities, like Griffin Creek and Grande-Ourse, are so weakened that their demise is clearly imminent. Macklin and Saint-Joachin, on the other hand, turn in on themselves, rejecting the outsider who brought new ideas with him, and, in this way, they survive.

Peculiarly suited to the history and traditions of Quebec, the theme of the disruptive visitor has been cultivated by Quebec writers for more than half a century. As the novels published in the last decade of the last century bear witness, it is far from exhausted and will no doubt continue to inspire future generations of novelists who will introduce their own variations.

Select Bibliography

Texts

BESSETTE, G., *Le Libraire*, Montréal: CLF, Poche Canadien, Le Cercle du Livre de France, 1968, (first published 1960).
GUÈVREMONT, G., *En Pleine Terre*, Montréal: Editions Paysana, 1942. References to Fides, 1976.
- *Le Survenant*, Montréal: Fides, Bibliothèque québécoise, 1986, chronologie, bibliographie et jugements critiques d'Aurélien Boivin, mis à jour (octobre 1984). This edition follows the revised text which Madame Guèvremont completed shortly before her death in 1968.
- *Marie-Didace*, Montréal: Fides, Bibliothèque québécoise, 1980, chronologie, bibliographie et jugements critiques d'Aurélien Boivin.
HAMELIN, L., *Cowboy*, Montréal: XYZ éditeur, 1992.
HÉBERT, A., *Les Fous de Bassan*, Paris: Seuil, 1982.
LANGEVIN, A., *Poussière sur la ville*, Montréal: Pierre Tisseyre, 1988. Originally published by Le Cercle du livre de France, 1953.
ROY, G., *Bonheur d'occasion*, Montréal: Stanké, 1977. Originally published by la Société des éditions, Pascal, 1945, 2 vols.

Translations

GUÈVREMONT, G., *The Outlander*. Translated by Eric Sutton, Toronto: McGraw Hill of Canada Limited, 1950.
- *Monk's Reach*, London: Evans Bros., 1950. (Both translations include *Marie-Didace*).

Critical Works

BARRACLOUGH, G., *The Times Atlas of World History*, edited by Geoffrey Barraclough, London: Times Books, 1978
BESSETTE G., *Trois romanciers québécois*, Montréal: Editions du jour, 1973.
DUCROCQ-POIRIER, M., *Le Roman canadien de langue française de 1860 à 1958*, Paris: Nizet, 1978.
DUFAULT, R.L., *Women By Women; The Treatment of Female Characters by Women Writers of Fiction in Quebec since 1980*. Madison: Fairleigh Dickinson University Press & London: Associated University Press, 1997.

DUMONT, F., *Genèse de la société québécoise*, Montréal: Boréal, 1996.
DUMONT, F. ET J.-C. FALARDEAU, *Littérature et société canadiennes-françaises*, Québec: Les Presses de l'Université Laval, 1964.
FRENETTE, Y., *Brève histoire des Canadiens français*, avec la collaboration de Martin Pâquet, Montréal: Boréal, 1998.
KEITH, W.J. AND B.-Z. SHEK, *The Arts in Canada*, Toronto: University of Toronto Press, 1980, (in particular the chapters by Guy Rocher, Gérard Bessette and Jacques Allard).
LAVOIE, M., 'Du coureur de bois au survenant; filiation ou aliénation?', *Voix et Images du Pays*, 3, 1970, 11-25.
LELAND, M., 'Quebec Literature in its American Context', in *The Canadian Imagination*, ed. Douglas Staines, Cambridge, Mass. and London: Harvard University Press, 1977, pp.188-225.
LEWIS, P.G., *Traditionalism, Nationalism, and Feminism: Women Writers of Quebec* edited by Paula Gilbert Lewis, Westport and London: Greenwood Press, 1985.
MAILHOT, L., *La Littérature québécoise depuis ses origines*, Montréal: Typo, 1997.
MARCOTTE, G., *Une Littérature qui se fait*, Montréal: Les Éditions HMH, 1962.
PARADIS, S., *Femme fictive, femme réelle*, Ottawa: Garneau, 1966.
ROBIDOUX, R., ET A. RENARD, *Le Roman canadien-français du vingtième siècle,* Ottawa: Les Éditions de l'Université d'Ottawa, 1966.
ROY, P.-E., *Études littéraires*, Montréal: Méridien Littérature, 1989.
SHEK B.-Z., *French-Canadian and Québécois Novels*, Toronto: Oxford University Press, 1991.
VANASSE, A., 'La Notion de l'étranger dans la littérature canadienne IV - La Rupture définitive', *L'Action Nationale*, 55, no.5, janvier, 1966, 606-11.
VERREAULT, R., *L'autre côté du monde*, Montréal: Liber, 1998.

Bessette

ALLARD, J., '*Le Libraire* de Gérard Bessette, ou comment la parole vient au pays du silence', *Voix et images du pays*, 1, 1970, 51-63.
BISHOP, D., 'A Novel of the Week', *The Ottawa Journal*, February 10, 1962.

CRONIN, M., 'Le Vertige et le dépassement de soi: les écrans alcooliques de Gérard Bessette', *Études canadiennes*, décembre 35, 1993, 189-204.
FRAPPIER, L., 'Le Livre en mouvement: du *Libraire* au *Semestre*', *Études françaises*, Spring 29:1, 1993, 61-74.
FRENCH, W., 'Quebec Novelist satirizes Censors', *Globe and Mail*, January 27, 1962, p. 15.
LAPIERRE, L., 'L'Ironie dans *Le Libraire* et *La Commensale* de Gérard Bessette', *Initiales*, 15, 1996, 25-41.
MARSHALL, J., 'A Satire set in Quebec', *The Windsor Star*, February, 20, 1962.
PICCIONE, M.-L., 'De quelques tavernes de la fiction québécoise', *Études canadiennes*, 35, décembre, 1993, 189-97.
RAOUL, V., *Distinctly Narcissistic: Diary Fiction in Quebec*, Toronto, Buffalo, London: University of Toronto Press, 1993, pp. 167-78.
ROBIDOUX, R., 'Gérard Bessette ou l'exaltation de la parole', *University of Toronto Quarterly*, 63, 4, 1994, Summer, 538-50.
SHEK, B.-Z., 'Gérard Bessette and Social Realism', *Canadian Modern Language Review*, 31, 1975, 292-300.
SHORTLIFFE, G., 'Evolution of a Novelist: Gérard Bessette', *Queen's Quarterly*, 74, 1967, 36-60.

Guèvremont

ALLARD, J., 'Deux scènes médianes où le discours prend corps', *Études françaises*, 33, 3, 1997, 53-66.
BAILLIE R., *Le Survenant; Lecture d'une passion*, Montréal: XYZ éditeur, 1999.
CHARBONNEAU, A., *Le Survenant: Germaine Guèvremont*, Montréal: Editions Hurtubise (Collection Texto HMH Français 4), 1997.
CIMON R., *Germaine Guèvremont*, Montréal: Fides, Dossiers de documentation sur la littérature canadienne-française, Vol. 5, 1969.
DUQUETTE, J.-P., *Germaine Guèvremont, une route, une maison*, Montréal: Les Presses de l'Université de Montréal, 1973.
GIROUARD, P., *Germaine Guèvremont et son oeuvre cachée*, (2me édition revue et corrigée) St. Ours, Québec: Les Éditions de Neveurmagne, 1985.

GREEN, M.-J., 'Gabrielle Roy and Germaine Guèvremont: Quebec's Daughters face a changing world', *Journal of Women's Studies in Literature*, Vol.1, no.3, Summer, 1979, 243-57.

HERLAN, J.J., '*Le Survenant* as Ideological Messenger: A Study of Germaine Guèvremont's Radio Serial' in *Traditionalism, Nationalism, and Feminism: Women Writers of Quebec* edited by Paula Gilbert Lewis, Westport and London: Greenwood Press, 1985, 37-52.

LECLERC, R., *Germaine Guèvremont*, Ottawa: Fides, Écrivains canadiens d'aujourd'hui, 1963.

LEPAGE, Y.G., *Germaine Guèvremont: la tentation autobiographique*, Ottawa: Les Presses de l'Université d'Ottawa, 1998.

LEPAGE, Y.G., 'L'Illusion réaliste dans *Le Survenant* de Germaine Guèvremont,' *Mélanges de littérature canadienne-française et québécoise offerts à Réjean Robidoux; textes réunis par Yolande Grisé et Robert Major*, Ottawa: Les Presses de l'Université d'Ottawa, 'Cahiers du CRCCF', 1992, pp.152-63.

MACCABEE-IQBAL, F., '"Survenant" le rédempteur' in *Solitude rompue: textes réunis par Cécile Cloutier-Wojciechowska et Réjean Robidoux en hommage à David M. Haynes*, Ottawa: Éditions de l'Université d'Ottawa, 1986, 248-56.

MAJOR, R., 'Le Survenant et la figure d'Eros dans l'œuvre de Germaine Guèvremont,' *Voix et Images*, décembre 2, no.2, 1976, 195-208.

MARCOTTE, G., '"Restons traditionnels et progressifs" disait Onésime Gagnon', *Études françaises*, 33, 3, 1997, 5-14.

MORENCY, J., 'Deux Visions de l'Amérique', *Études françaises*, 33, 3, 1997, 67-77.

PARIZEAU, A., 'Germaine Guèvremont, écrivain du Québec', *La Presse*, 3 février, 1968, 12-15.

SAINT-MARTIN, L., 'Sexe, pouvoir et dialogue,' *Études françaises*, 33, 3, 1997, 37-52.

SERVAIS-MAQUOI, M., *Le Roman de la terre au Québec*, Québec: Les Presses de l'Université Laval, 1974.

SMART, P., *Writing in the Father's House*, Toronto, Buffalo and London: University of Toronto Press, 1991.

THÉRIO, A., 'Le Survenant de Germaine Guèvremont', *Lettres québécoises*, 1982-3, 28, Hiver, 25-28.

VANASSE, A., 'La Notion de l'étranger dans la littérature canadienne IV - la rupture définitive', *L'Action Nationale*, 55 no. 5, janvier, 1966, 606-11.

VAUCHERET, E., 'Deux Conceptions du "Survenant" chez Jean Giono et Germaine Guèvremont', *Études Canadiennes*, 8, 1980, 47-60.
WILLIAMSON, R., 'The Stranger within: sexual politics in the Novels of Germaine Guèvremont', *Quebec Studies*, Vol.1, no. 1, printemps, 1983, 246-56.

Hamelin

ALLARD, J., 'La nuit amérindienne', *Le Devoir*, samedi 17 octobre 1992, D-3.
ALLARD, J., *Le Roman mauve*, Montréal: Québec/Amérique, 1997, pp.54-6.
COTE, L., 'Louis Hamelin, un étranger au *Far-West québécois*, *La Presse*, Montréal, dimanche 4 octobre 1992, B1,4.
FORTIN, M.-C., Le Temps d'une chasse', *Voir*, du 8 au 14 octobre, 1992, 12-13.
NOBLE, P.S., 'Fracture et rupture dans le Nord de Québec dans l'oeuvre de Louis Hamelin', *Caliban*, 1, 1997, 115-122.
ROYER, J., Après le cri de rage, le cri d'épouvante', *Le Devoir*, 23 février 1991, D 1.
RUGGERI, P., '*Cowboy* de Louis Hamelin; Le *Far West* québécois ou la rédéfinition des frontières' *Globe*, 1; 2, 1998. 9-27.

Hébert

ALLARD, J., 'La chambre des rêves; aspects du récit amoureux dans *Les Fous de Bassan*' in *Mélanges de littérature canadienne-française et québécoise offerts à Réjean Robidoux; textes réunis par Yolande Grisé et Robert Major*, Ottawa: Les Presses de l'Université d'Ottawa, "Cahiers du CRCCF", 1992, 5-15.
BACKÈS, J.-L., 'Le retour des morts dans l'oeuvre d'Anne Hébert', *Esprit créateur*, XXIII, 3, automne 1983, 48-57.
BISHOP, N.B., 'Distance, point de vue, voix et idéologie dans *Les Fous de Bassan* d'Anne Hébert', *Voix et Images*, 9, no. 2, hiver 1984, 113-129.
BISHOP, N.B., 'Energie textuelle et production de sens: images de l'énergie dans *les Fous de Bassan* d'Anne Hébert', *University of Toronto Quarterly*, LIV, hiver, 1984-85, 178-99.
BISHOP, N.B., *Anne Hébert, son oeuvre, leurs exils*, Bordeaux: Les Presses universitaires de Bordeaux, 1993.

BISHOP, N.B., 'Guerre, errances et exils dans l'œuvre d'Anne Hébert', *Anne Hébert, parcours d'une œuvre, Actes du colloque de la Sorbonne.* Montréal: l'Hexagone, 1997, 163-74.
BOYCE, M.-D., Création de la mère/mer: symbole du paradis perdu dans *Les Fous de Bassan*', *The French Review*, 68, no. 2, December, 1994, 294-302.
CAUCHON, P., 'Simoneau et *Les Fous de Bassan:* "On a fait un contre les vagues..." '*Le Devoir,* 28 juillet 1986, C-1 et C-4.
CHEVILLOT, F., 'Tradition et modernité: histoire, narration et récit dans *Les Fous de Bassan* d'Anne Hébert', *Quebec Studies*, 9, 1989-90, 121-130.
CÔTÉ, P.R. AND MITCHELL, C., '*Les Fous de Bassan* and *Le Torrent:* At the Crossroads of Desire and Delusion', *Modern Language Studies*, Fall, 21, 4, 1991, 78-89.
DUCROCQ-POIRIER, M., *Anne Hébert, parcours d'une œuvre, Actes du colloque de la Sorbonne.* Montréal: l'Hexagone, 1997.
EWING, R., 'The English World of Griffin Creek', *Canadian Literature*, 105, été 1985, 100-110.
FRANCOLI, Y., 'Griffin Creek: refuge des *Fous de Bassan* et bessons fous, *Etudes littéraires*, XVII, no.1, avril, 1984, 131-42.
GASQUY-RESCH, Y., *Littérature du Québec,* Vanves: EDICEF / AUPELF, 1994.
GONTARD, M., 'Noir, blanc et rouge: le chromo-roman d'Anne Hébert', in *Anne Hébert, parcours d'une œuvre, Actes du colloque de la Sorbonne.* Montréal: l'Hexagone, 1997, 251-64.
GOSSELIN, M., 'Le Ravissement de l'enfance dans les récits d'Anne Hébert', in *Anne Hébert, parcours d'une œuvre, Actes du colloque de la Sorbonne.* Montréal: l'Hexagone, 1997, 119-30.
GOULD, K., 'Absence and Meaning in Anne Hébert's *les Fous de Bassan*', *French Review*, LIX, 6, mai 1986, 921-30.
GUILLEMETTE, L., 'Pour une nouvelle lecture des *Fous de Bassan* d'Anne Hébert: l'Amérique et ses parcours discursifs', *Voix et Images*, 22, 2, hiver, 1997, 334-54.
HARLIN, L., 'Unreliable Views of the Feminine in Anne Hébert's *Les Fous de Bassan*', *Quebec Studies*, 21-22, 1996,127-136.
HILLENAAR, H., 'Anne Hébert et le "roman familial" de Freud' in *Le roman québécois depuis 1960* sous la direction de Louise Milot et Jaap Lintvelt, Sainte-Foy: Les Presses de l'Université de Laval, 1992.
KNIGHT, K.W., *Anne Hébert: In Search of the First Garden*, New York: Peter Lang, 1998.

KROGNES, H.S., 'Une voix organisatrice dans *Les fous de Bassan* d'Anne Hébert', *Tribune*, 10, Autumn, 1999, 83-99.
LAMY, S., 'Le Roman de l'irresponsabilité', *Spirale*, 29, novembre 1982, 2-3
LEE, S., 'La Rhétorique de la folie: métaphore et allégorie dans *Les Fous de Bassan*', *Voix et Images*, 19, 2, hiver, 1994, 374-93.
LOUETTE, P., 'Les voix/voies du désir dans *Les Fous de Bassan* d'Anne Hébert (1982)', in *Anne Hébert, parcours d'une œuvre, Actes du colloque de la Sorbonne*. Montréal: l'Hexagone, 1997, 307-24.
MARCOTTE, G., '*Les Fous de Bassan*: le grand roman de la rentrée', *L'Actualité* 7, 10, 1982, 129.
MELANÇON, R., 'Anne Hébert: ce qui est sans nom ni date', *Liberté*, 145, février 1983, 89-93.
MERLER, G., '*Les Fous de Bassan* d'Anne Hébert devant la critique', *Oeuvres et Critiques*, XIV 1, 1989, 39-44.
MÉSAVAGE, R., 'L'herméneutique de l'écriture: *les Fous de Bassan* d'Anne Hébert', *Québec Studies*, no.5, 1987, 113-23.
NOBLE, P. S., 'The Thirties in Anne Hébert and Antonine Maillet', *London Journal of Canadian Studies*, 8, 1992, 28-35.
NOBLE, P.S., *Anne Hébert: Les Fous de Bassan*, Glasgow: University of Glasgow French and German Publications, 36, 1995.
O'REILLY, M., 'Le jeu des rhythmes dans *Les Fous de Bassan*', *Canadian Literature*, summer, 1992, 133, 109-128.
OUELLETTE-MICHALSKA, M., 'Anne Hébert. L'attrait du double'. *Le Devoir*, 11 septembre 1982, 17 & 32.
PATERSON, J.M., 'L'envolée de l'écriture: *les Fous de Bassan* d'Anne Hébert', *Voix et Images*, IX, 3 printemps 1984, 143-151.
PATERSON, J.M., *Anne Hébert: architecture romanesque*, Ottawa: Éditions de l'Université d'Ottawa, 1985.
POULIN, G., 'L'écriture enchantée: *les Fous de Bassan* d'Anne Hébert', *Lettres québécoises*, 28, hiver 1982-83, 15-18.
RANDALL, M., 'Les énigmes des *Fous de Bassan*: féminisme, narration et clôture', *Voix et Images*, 43, automne, 1989, 66-82.
REID, G., 'Wind in August: *Les Fous de Bassan's* Reply to Faulkner', *Studies in Canadian Literature*, 16, 2, 1991, 112-27.
REA, A., 'The Climate of Viol/Violence and Madness in Anne Hébert's *Les Fous de Bassan*', *Québec Studies* 4, 1986, 170-83.
REA, A., 'Les Jardins d'Anne Hébert', in *Anne Hébert, parcours d'une œuvre, Actes du colloque de la Sorbonne*. Montréal: l'Hexagone, 1997, 325-38.

ROY, L., *Entre la lumière et l'ombre. L'Univers poétique d'Anne Hébert*, Sherbrooke: Éditions Naaman, 1984.
SASU, V., 'Crimes et châtiments dans les romans et récits d'Anne Hébert' in *Anne Hébert, parcours d'une œuvre, Actes du colloque de la Sorbonne*. Montréal: l'Hexagone, 1997, 175-84.
SENÉCAL, A.J., '*Les Fous de Bassan*: an Eschatology', *Québec Studies*, 7, 1988, 150-60.
SIROIS, A., 'Bible, mythes et *Fous de Bassan* d'Anne Hébert', *Canadian Literature*, 104, printemps 1985, 178-82.
SIROIS, A,. 'Anne Hébert et la Bible', *Voix et Images*, 39, printemps, 1988, 459-72.
SIROIS, A., 'L'Initiation dans les récits d'Anne Hébert', in *Anne Hébert, parcours d'une œuvre, Actes du colloque de la Sorbonne*. Montréal: l'Hexagone, 1997, 131-38.
SLOTT, K., 'Submersion and Resurgence of the Female Other in Anne Hébert's *Les Fous de Bassan*', *Québec Studies*, 4, 1986, 158-69.
SLOTT, K., 'Repression, Obsession and Re-emergence in Hébert's *Les Fous de Bassan*', *American Review of Canadian Studies*, XVII, 3, 1987, 297-307.
STEPHAN, A., 'Le Règne de l'eau dans *Les Fous de Bassan* d'Anne Hébert', *Études canadiennes*, 27, 1989, 116-22.

Langevin

AMPRIMOZ, A.L., '*Poussière sur la ville*: l'animalité d'un personnage', *Studies in Canadian Literature*, 10, 1-2, 1985, 154-61.
AMPRIMOZ, A.L., '*Poussière sur la ville* vers une sémiotique de gestes', *Présence Francophone*, Printemps, 14, 1977, 97-104.
BEAVER, J., 'La Métaphore théâtrale dans l'œuvre romanesque d'André Langevin', *Études littéraires*, 6, no. 2 août, 1973, 169-97.
BEDNARSKI, B., 'Espace et fatalité dans *Poussière sur la ville*', *Études littéraires*, 6, no. 2 août, 1973, 215-39.
BOND, D.J., *The Temptation of Despair*, Fredericton, N.B.: York Press, 1982 (Introduction, Chapter 2 and Conclusion).
BROCHU, A., '*Poussière sur la ville*: le destin n'était pas au rendez-vous', *Revue d'histoire littéraire du Québec et du Canada français*, Winter-Spring, 11, 1986, 57-66.
BROCHU, A., *L'évasion tragique; Essai sur les romans d'André Langevin*, Lavalle: Hurtubise HMH, 1985.

DORÉ, M., *Poussière sur la ville; André Langevin*, Montréal: Editions Hurtubise (Collections Texto HMH, Francais 5), 1998.

FALARDEAU, J.-C., 'Les Milieux sociaux dans le roman canadien-français contemporain' in *Littérature et société canadiennes-françaises*, edited by Fernand Dumont and Jean-Charles Falardeau, Québec: Les Presses de l'Université Laval, 1964, 123-44.

FILIATRAUT, J., 'Quelques manifestations de la révolte dans notre littérature récente', in *Littérature et société canadiennes-françaises*, edited by Fernand Dumont and Jean-Charles Falardeau, Québec: Les Presses de l'Université Laval, 1964, 177-90.

GAULIN, A., 'La Vision du monde d'André Langevin', *Études littéraires*, 6, no. 2 août, 1973, 153-67.

HEBERT, P., *Le Temps et la forme*, Sherbrooke: Éditions Naaman, 1983.

MARCOTTE, G., 'La Religion dans la littérature canadienne-française contemporaine' in *Littérature et société canadiennes-françaises*, edited by Fernand Dumont and Jean-Charles Falardeau, Québec: Les Presses de l'Université Laval, 1964, 167-76.

PASCAL, G., *La Quête de l'identité chez André Langevin*, Montréal: Éditions Aquila, 1976.

PICCIONE, M.-L., 'Le Symbolisme de la machine chez André Langevin', *Études canadiennes*, 8, 1980, 65-75.

SOCKEN, P., 'Alain Dubois's Commitment: a Reading of *Poussière sur la ville*', *International Fiction Review*, 4, 1977, 174-77.

TARDIF, J.-C., 'Les Relations humaines dans *Poussière sur la ville*', *Études littéraires*, 6, no. 2 août, 1973, 241-55.

TELLIER, C., 'Les conflits idéologiques dans *Poussière sur la ville*', *Voix et Images*, 22, 3 printemps, 1997, 569-81.

VOISINE, S., 'L'Expression de l'espace dans la trilogie romanesque d'André Langevin', *Études littéraires*, 6, no. 2 août, 1973, 199-213.